THE WHOLE PSYCHOLOGY CATALOG

A potpourri of lecture outlines, articles, activities, quizzes, transparency masters, and other handouts for introductory psychology

Prepared by

Deborea Winfrey
Winston-Salem State University

Holt, Rinehart and Winston, Inc.

Fort Worth   Chicago   San Francisco   Philadelphia
Montreal   Toronto   London   Sydney   Tokyo

Address for Editorial correspondence: Holt, Rinehart and Winston, Inc., 301 Commerce Street, Suite 3700 Fort Worth, Texas 76102

ISBN 0-03-030429-6

Printed in the United States of America

0 1 2 3   017   9 8 7 6 5 4 3 2 1

Holt, Rinehart and Winston, Inc.
The Dryden Press
Saunders College Publishing

CONTENTS

Introduction

Chapter 1: What is Psychology?

Handout 1.1 — The Science of Psychology
Handout 1.2 — Historical Schools of Psychology
Handout 1.3 — Anatomy of an Experiment
Handout 1.4 — The Psychological Viewpoint Questionnaire
Handout 1.5 — *When Laws and Values Conflict: A Dilemma for Psychologists* (article)

Chapter 2: Biology and Behavior

Handout 2.1 — Nature Versus Nurture
Handout 2.2 — An Overview of the Nervous System
Handout 2.3 — Functions of the Autonomic Nervous System
Handout 2.4 — Primary Structures of the Human Brain
Handout 2.5 — Major Areas of the Cerebral Cortex
Handout 2.6 — A Quiz on Glands and Hormones
Handout 2.7 — An Overview of Genetics
Handout 2.8 — Dominant and Recessive Characteristics
Handout 2.9 — *The Shockley Case* (article)
Handout 2.10 — *Genes and Behavior: A Twin Legacy* (article)

Chapter 3: Sensation and Perception

Handout 3.1 — An Overview of Sensation and Perception
Handout 3.2 — An Overview of Sensory Processes
Handout 3.3 — The Human Eye
Handout 3.4 — Visual Illusions
Handout 3.5 — Gestalt Principles of Organization
Handout 3.6 — Reversible Figure – Ground Patterns
Handout 3.7 — The Human Ear
Handout 3.8 — The Organ of Corti
Handout 3.9 — The Taste Receptors
Handout 3.10 — The Olfaction Receptors
Handout 3.11 — Receptors for the Skin Senses
Handout 3.12 — *The President's Speech* (article)
Handout 3.13 — *Phenomena, Comment, and Notes* (article)

Chapter 4: States of Consciousness

Handout 4.1 — Sleep: Approaches and Issues
Handout 4.2 — An Overview of Drug-Related Behaviors
Handout 4.3 — An Overview of Drugs

Handout 4.4 — A Summary Chart of Drugs and Their Effects
Handout 4.5 — Quiz: How Much Do You Know About Crack and Cocaine?
Handout 4.6 — *The Stuff of Dreams* (article)

Chapter 5: *Learning*

Handout 5.1 — An Overview of Learning Theories
Handout 5.2 — An Overview of Classical Conditioning
Handout 5.3 — An Overview of Operant Conditioning
Handout 5.4 — The Effects of Reinforcers and Punishment
Handout 5.5 — Behavior Patterns Resulting from Different Reinforcement Schedules
Handout 5.6 — *The Slow Rise of a Rapid-Learning System* (article)

Chapter 6: *Memory*

Handout 6.1 — An Overview of Memory Processes
Handout 6.2 — A Simple Recollection Test
Handout 6.3 — Paired Associates
Handout 6.4 — *Variety, The Spice of Memory* (article)
Handout 6.5 — *Weakened Memories, But Sound Minds* (article)

Chapter 7: *Language, Thought, and Intelligence*

Handout 7.1 — An Overview of Language
Handout 7.2 — Language Structure: Definitions and Examples
Handout 7.3 — Two Problems to Solve
Handout 7.4 — An Overview of Intelligence
Handout 7.5 — *Is Thinking Unconscious?* (article)
Handout 7.6 — *Waking Sleeping Souls: The Quiet Revolution in Down's Syndrome* (article)

Chapter 8: *Motivation and Emotion*

Handout 8.1 — An Overview of Motivation
Handout 8.2 — Maslow's Hierarchy of Needs
Handout 8.3 — Counting Calories
Handout 8.4 — An Overview of Social Motivation
Handout 8.5 — An Overview of Emotions
Handout 8.6 — *Why Kids Get Fat* (article)

Chapter 9: *Development*

Handout 9.1 — An Overview of Development
Handout 9.2 — Milestones of Infant Motor Development
Handout 9.3 — Piaget's Stages of Cognitive Development
Handout 9.4 — Kohlberg's Stages of Moral Development
Handout 9.5 — Three Moral Dilemmas
Handout 9.6 — Erikson's Stages of Psychosocial Development
Handout 9.7 — Attitudes Toward Aging Test

Handout 9.8 — Facts on Aging
Handout 9.9 — Kubler-Ross: The Five Phases of Dying
Handout 9.10 — *Preventing Early Births: Prenatal Care Not Only Works, It's a Bargain* (article)

Chapter 10: Personality

Handout 10.1 — An Overview of Personality Theories
Handout 10.2 — Behavior Determinants Test
Handout 10.3 — Freud's Model of Personality
Handout 10.4 — Freud's Stages of Psychosexual Development
Handout 10.5 — Common Ego Defense Mechanisms
Handout 10.6 — Measuring Self-Actualization
Handout 10.7 — An Overview of Assessment
Handout 10.8 — Inkblots Similar to Those Used in the Rorschach Test
Handout 10.9 — *Personality — Is it All in Your Genes?* (article)
Handout 10.10 — *Personality's Part and Parcel* (article)

Chapter 11: Health Psychology

Handout 11.1 — An Overview of Stress
Handout 11.2 — The College Schedule of Recent Experiences
Handout 11.3 — Taking a STABS at It: The (Abbreviated) Suinn Test Anxiety Behavior Scale
Handout 11.4 — Conflict Type Identification: A Matching Exercise
Handout 11.5 — Full-Length Progressive Relaxation Instructions
Handout 11.6 — *How Psychological Factors Can Cause Physical Illness* (article)

Chapter 12: Abnormal Psychology

Handout 12.1 — An Overview of Abnormality
Handout 12.2 — DSM III-R Classifications (Condensed)
Handout 12.3 — Zung's Self-Rating Depression Scale
Handout 12.4 — An Overview of Depression
Handout 12.5 — Durkheim's Classification of Suicide
Handout 12.6 — *The Struggle of Kitty Dukakis* (article)

Chapter 13: Therapies

Handout 13.1 — An Overview of Psychotherapy
Handout 13.2 — A Primer on the Professions
Handout 13.3 — An Overview of Psychoanalysis
Handout 13.4 — An Overview of Behavior Therapy
Handout 13.5 — An Overview of Cognitive Therapy
Handout 13.6 — Using Assertive Behavior to Get a Job
Handout 13.7 — *Talk Is as Good as a Pill* (article)
Handout 13.8 — *In Massachusetts: Theatre Therapy* (article)

Chapter 14: Human Sexuality

Handout 14.1 — An Overview of Human Sexuality
Handout 14.2 — Male and Female Sexual Response Patterns
Handout 14.3 — *On the Trail of the Big O* (article)
Handout 14.4 — Psychosexual Disorders
Handout 14.5 — Love, Sex, and You: A Quiz on AIDS
Handout 14.6 — *Latest Infertility Suspect: Caffeine* (article)
Handout 14.7 — *Birth Control: New Approval for a 19th Century Technique* (article)

Chapter 15: Social Psychology

Handout 15.1 — An Overview of Attitudes
Handout 15.2 — Social Perception Survey
Handout 15.3 — An Overview of Social Perception
Handout 15.4 — An Overview of Social Facilitation
Handout 15.5 — *Mind If I Cut In?* (article)

Chapter 16: Applied Psychology

Handout 16.1 — An Overview of Applied Psychology
Handout 16.2 — *The Moral Implications of Nutritional Therapy: Is Controlling Behavior Through Diet a Humanistic Alternative to Incarceration?* (article)

Chapter 17: Statistics

Handout 17.1 — An Overview of Statistics
Handout 17.2 — The Normal Distribution

INTRODUCTION

The students enrolled in an introductory psychology course are often pursuing answers to several questions. On the one hand they are seeking to understand the fundamental concepts and theories that serve as the underpinnings for the discipline. In addition, some students are making a threshold appraisal of psychology as their career choice. These students are asking of the discipline, "What can I expect as challenges and opportunities from a career in psychology?"

The WHOLE PSYCHOLOGY CATALOG was developed to enrich the explorations into these questions.

Several media are used in the catalogue's materials to facilitate an enlightening learning experience. Each unit begins with an overview, in chart or diagram form, which summarizes key concepts and the relationships between them. Supporting articles from a variety of popular and professional sources are provided to present a diversity of perspectives and philosophies on central topic areas. Where appropriate, graphs and other illustrative materials are included to help achieve the maximum conceptual understanding. Discussion questions at the conclusion of most readings are designed to encourage the student's knowledgeable expression of relevant concepts and theories as well as to stimulate an active comparison, contrast, and synthesis of different outlooks.

The catalog also includes experiential exercises in recognition of the fact that the best and most lasting insights are derived from learning by doing. These exercises have been designed to be educational as well as fun. You will find both collegial small group and individual learning activities here. These reinforce and expand the student's learning by actually allowing the student to work with the theories and concepts within discussions, problem-solving situations, and other simulated activities.

Instructors are encouraged to creatively and collectively use these materials as handouts, quizzes, or assignments to derive the most effective course experience for each class.

We would welcome any feedback on the utility of these materials, including suggestions for improvement, as well as any other comments.

Deborea Winfrey
August, 1989

Chapter 1
What is Psychology?

THE SCIENCE OF PSYCHOLOGY

Definition of Psychology	The scientific study of behavior and mental processes
Goals of Psychology	To understand, predict, and control (modify) behavior and mental processes

Tools of Psychology	Scientific Method
	  Observation
	  Defining a Problem
	  Proposing a Hypothesis
	  Experimentation
	  Theory Formulation

HISTORICAL SCHOOLS OF PSYCHOLOGY

Name	Main People	Main Goals
Structuralism	Titchener	Study the elements of consciousness
Functionalism	James Hall Dewey	Study the functions of the mind, not its elements
Gestalt Psychology	Wertheimer Kohler	Study perception and cognitive behavior as a whole; they cannot be understood by breaking them into parts
Psychoanalysis	Freud Adler	Understand personality by studying the underlying drives and motivations that shape it from childhood
Behaviorism	Watson Skinner	The study of observable behavior, not consciousness, is the proper subject matter of psychology

ANATOMY OF AN EXPERIMENT

This is an outline of a simple psychological experiment which could be used to assess the effects of noise during study on test scores.

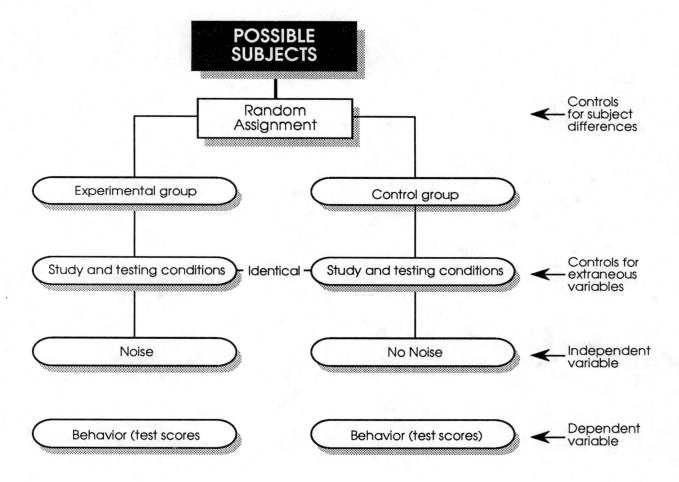

THE PSYCHOLOGICAL VIEWPOINT QUESTIONNAIRE

Psychologist William R. Miller of the University of New Mexico has constructed a Psychological Viewpoint Questionnaire which you can use to clarify some of your beliefs about human nature. It will also tell you with what major psychological theories you are likely to find yourself in sympathy as you read this chapter.

Read each of the following statements and decide whether you agree more than disagree, or disagree more than agree, with each one. Write an "A" next to those statements with which you agree more than disagree, and write "D" next to those statements with which you disagree more than agree. Express your opinion about every statement even though you may have some trouble deciding in some cases.

_____ 1. In attempting to understand human beings, one should stick to what can be directly observed and avoid theory or concepts that cannot be seen or observed.

_____ 2. Events taking place in the present are systematically linked to events that have occurred in one's past.

_____ 3. A specific piece of human behavior cannot be understood without considering the person and his or her life as a whole.

_____ 4. People are basically good (as opposed to neutral or evil). If left to a natural state without external controls, they seek health and personal growth while respecting the right of others to do the same.

_____ 5. A person's character is largely determined before he or she reaches adulthood. The only changes that one can expect an adult are relatively small ones, and these occur slowly over long periods of time.

_____ 6. General laws of behavior and experience that apply to all people are not very helpful if you want to understand a particular individual.

_____ 7. Much behavior, both normal and abnormal, is directed by unconscious impulses and motivations.

_____ 8. Aggression is an inherent and inescapable part of human nature.

_____ 9. People are capable of making major and lasting changes in themselves within a relatively brief period of time.

_____ 10. Human behavior can be understood as a continuous attempt to increase pleasure and to avoid pain and discomfort.

_____ 11. There are no values inherent in human nature or the human condition — only those that are discovered or learned through experience.

_____ 12. Learning processes play a major determining role in the formation of personality and human behavior.

_____ 13. Events that occur early in life are more important in determining one's adult personality and behavior than are similar events occurring after the person has reached adulthood.

_____ 14. Looking inside a person for the causes of behavior (for needs, impulses, motivations, etc.) is probably more misleading than enlightening.

_____ 15. The use of scientific experiments is not an appropriate way to try to understand the psychology of human beings.

_____ 16. People are neither inherently good nor basically selfish.

_____ 17. In order to change a present pattern of behavior, it is important for the person to explore the past, particularly childhood, to find the causes of the behavior.

_____ 18. Little or none of what people do is the result of free will. Behavior is controlled by lawful principles, and free choice is an illusion.

_____ 19. The therapist who wants to help a person change should not direct advice or suggestions. Rather, the best approach is for the therapist to allow the person to talk and explore his or her feelings without direction or evaluation.

_____ 20. A person is free to be what he or she wants to be.

SCORING THE PSYCHOLOGICAL VIEWPOINT QUESTIONNAIRE

Below are twenty lines of letters corresponding to the twenty items of the PVQ. For each item, circle all of the A's in that row if you agreed with the statement or circle all of the D's in that row if you disagreed with the statement.

Items	B	E	H	P
1.	A	A	D	D
2.	A	D	D	A
3.	D	A	A	A
4.	D	D	A	D
5.	D	D	D	A
6.	D	A	A	D
7.	D	D	D	A
8.	D	D	D	A
9.	A	A	A	D
10.	A	D	D	A
11.	A	A	D	D
12.	A	D	D	A
13.	D	D	D	A
14.	A	D	D	D
15.	D	A	D	D
16.	A	A	D	D
17.	D	D	D	D
18.	A	D	D	A
19.	D	A	A	A
20.	D	A	A	D
Totals:	**B**	**E**	**H**	**P**

After you have coded your answers, count to see how many time you circled an "A" or "D" in each column and enter your totals at the bottom of the page. Which theoretical perspective did you agree with most — Behavioral (B), Existential (E), Humanistic (H), or Psychoanalytic (P)? Which viewpoint did you disagree with the most?

WHEN LAWS AND VALUES CONFLICT: A Dilemma for Psychologists

Kenneth S. Pope
Theresa Rose Bajt

Edmund Burke (1961) stated the importance of absolute compliance with the law: "One of the first motives to civil society, and which becomes one of its fundamental rules, is that **no man should be judge in his own cause**" (p. 71). The U.S. Supreme Court, in Walker v Birmingham (1967), underscored this "belief that in the fair administration of justice no man can be judge in his own case, however exalted his station, however righteous his motives, and irrespective of his race, color, politics, or religion" (pp. 1219 – 1220).

Henry David Thoreau (1960), however, urged that if a law "requires you to be the agent of injustice to another, then, I say, break the law" (p. 242). Even the California Supreme Court seemed to give tacit approval to breaking the law **as long as it is done within the framework of civil disobedience:** "If we were to deny to every person who has engaged in...nonviolent civil disobedience... the right to enter a licensed profession, we would deprive the community of the services of many highly qualified persons of the highest moral courage" (Hallinan v Committee of Bar Examiners of State Bar, 1966, p. 239).

Neither stance may seem acceptable to psychologists who believe that compliance with a legal or professional obligation would be harmful, unjust, or otherwise wrong. Absolute compliance connotes a "just following orders" mentality all too ready to sacrifice personal values and client welfare to an imperfect system of rules and regulations. Selective noncompliance connotes an association of people who have anointed themselves as somehow above the law, able to pick and choose which legal obligations and recognized standards they will obey.

Civil disobedience itself may be precluded in significant areas of psychology. Coined as a term by Thoreau, civil disobedience as a concept has been developed, defined, and justified as an act involving open and public violation of the law while volunteering to accept the legal penalties (Gandhi, 1948; King, 1958, 1964; Plato 1956a, 1956b; Thoreau, 1960; Tolstoy, 1951). This absolute openness—the lack of any attempt to avoid detection and prosecution—is essential in reaffirming respect for the process of law and accountability. But how can a psychologist, for example, publicly refuse to make a mandated report (e.g. regarding child abuse or potential harm to third parties) about a student, client, or subject without betraying the supposedly secret information?

We used an anonymous survey, with a 60% return rate, to explore this dilemma. The questionnaire was mailed to 100 senior psychologists, presumably acknowledged by their peers as knowledgeable and scrupulous regarding professional accountability: 60 current or former members of state ethics committees (50 of whom had served as chairs), 10 current or former members of the American Psychological Association (APA) Ethics Committee, 10 authors of textbooks focusing on legal or ethical aspects of psychology, and 20 diplomates of the American Board of Professional Psychology.

The first question was: "In the most serious, significant, or agonizing instance, if any, what law of formal ethical principle have you broken intentionally in light of a client's welfare or other deeper value?"

A majority (57%) acknowledged such instances. Of these 34 instances, the following were reported by more than one respondent: 7 (21%) involved refusing to report child abuse, 7 (32%) involved illegally divulging confidential information, 3 (9%) involved engaging in sex with a client, 2 (6%) involved "dual relationships" (no details), and 2 (6%) involved refusing to make legally mandated warnings regarding dangerous clients. It is interesting to note that 48% involve the issue of whether certain information should be kept confidential. It is dismaying to note that 9% involve psychologists' using "client welfare or other deeper value" as a rationale for engaging in sex with a client.

Incidents reported by one respondent each were giving a student an inappropriately high grade to "help" the student, helping a colleague to fake a credential, using one's professional status and expertise to help someone obtain an illegal abortion, committing perjury to keep a client from going to jail, engaging in "insurance fraud" (respondent's phrase) to help the client pay for services, treating a minor without parents' consent, refusing to turn over a former client's records in response to a legitimate request, accepting a very expensive gift from a client, withholding significant information from a patient, refusing to collect insurance co-payment, blurring a personal and professional relationship, continuing therapy beyond the point at which it should have ended, and "lied about my experience treating a particular disorder, in order to instill confidence in the patient to be."

Exactly half of the respondents consulted someone before taking the action; 68% discussed the incident afterwards. Beneficial results were reported by 91%; ill effects by 44%. Only one psychologist was, as a result of the incident, the object of a formal complaint. Seventy-three percent would, in hindsight, take the same action if the circumstances were the same.

Seventy-seven percent of the respondents believed "that formal legal and ethical standards should ever be violated on the basis of patient welfare or other deeper values." In light of the fact that three fourths of this select sample believed that psychologists should sometimes violate formal legal and ethical standards, and that a majority have actually done so, it is regrettable that only 18% report that the topic of conflicts between deeply held values and formal legal or ethical obligations was adequately addressed in their education, training and supervision, and that only 22% believe that the topic is adequately addressed in the professional literature.

Are the aims toward which our laws and formal ethical standards strive ultimately supported or subverted when psychologists intentionally violate explicit legal and ethical standards that conflict with the psychologists' deeply held values? How can psychologists who believe that the authority of the legal and ethical codes are not absolute ensure that their actions are based on sound professional judgment rather than on self-interest, prejudice, rationalization, and the sense that one is "above the law"? Are the integrity, effectiveness, and fairness of our mechanisms of accountability— such as university grievance committees, human subjects review committees, and ethics committees— enriched or eroded when those who sit in judgment on the behavior of others have themselves intentionally broken the rule that they are seeking to enforce? Such dilemmas are in need of open acknowledgment and serious study.

Discussion Questions

1. Should psychologists be mandated to follow professional or ethical rules which conflict with their personal beliefs? Why or why not?

2. Examining the single incidents listed above, discuss whether or not you believe that they constituted an ethical violation. Why or why not?

Chapter 2
Biology and Behavior

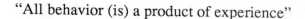

NATURE VERSUS NURTURE

"All behavior (is) a product of experience"

— Erasmus Darwin, *Zoonomia*

"Give me a dozen healthy infants, well-formed, and my own specified world to bring them up in and I'll guarantee to take any one at random and train him to become any type of specialist I might select — doctor, lawyer, artist, merchant-chief and, yes, even beggar-man and thief, regardless of his talents, penchants, tendencies, abilities, vocations, and race of his ancestors."

— J. B. Watson, *Behaviorism*

"I have no patience with the hypothesis occasionally expressed, and often implied, especially in tales written to teach children to be good, that babies are born pretty much alike, and the sole agencies in creating differences between boy and boy, and man and man, are steady application and moral "effort."

— Francis Galton, *Classification of Men According to Their Natural Gifts*

"I believe that the research, based on the study of twins and adopted children, of correlations between different degrees of kinship, and so on, established a strong genetic factor in individual differences in intelligence, and we shouldn't be surprised that different human groups that have been isolated breeding populations for centuries differ in mental as well as physical traits."

— Arthur Jensen, *The Making of Psychology*

AN OVERVIEW OF THE NERVOUS SYSTEM

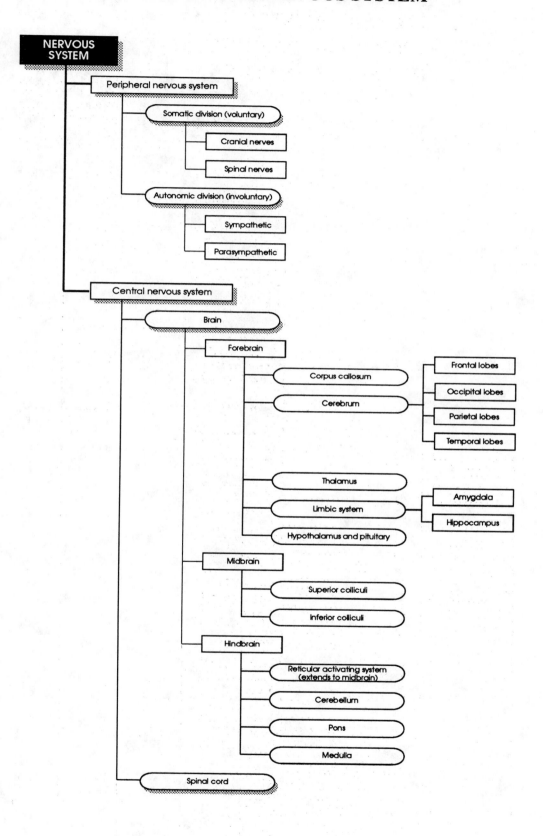

FUNCTIONS OF THE AUTONOMIC NERVOUS SYSTEM

Parasympathetic Functions	Sympathetic Functions
constricts pupils	dilates pupils
stimulates salivation	inhibits salivation
slows heartbeat	accelerates heartbeat
slows respiration	increases respiration
stimulates digestion	inhibits digestion
stimulates gall bladder	
	secretes adrenaline and noradrenaline
	stimulates glucose release
contracts bladder	relaxes bladder
stimulates genitals	inhibits genitals

PRIMARY STRUCTURES OF THE HUMAN BRAIN

Can you name all of the parts of the human brain shown here?

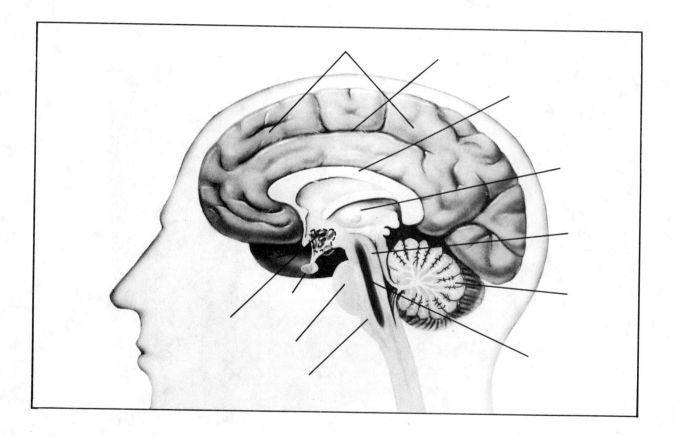

MAJOR AREAS OF THE CEREBRAL CORTEX

Complete the name of each part of the cerebral cortex shown below.

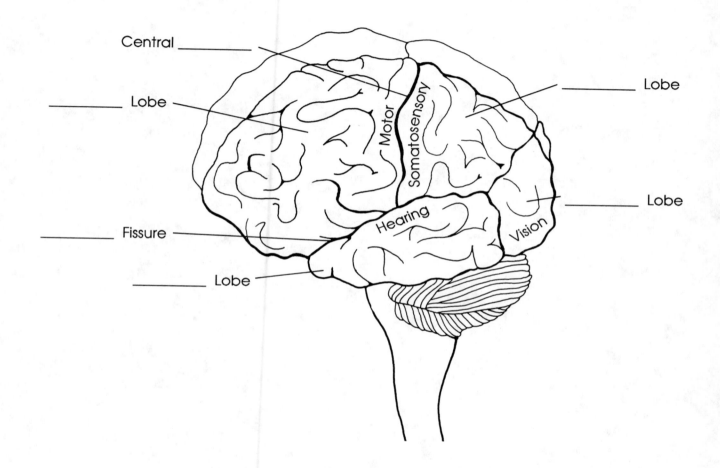

A QUIZ ON GLANDS AND HORMONES

Directions: Match the hormone with the gland that secretes it.

Hormone	Gland
_____ 1. Steroids	A. Anterior Pituitary
_____ 2. Adrenalin	B. Posterior Pituitary
_____ 3. Thyrotrophin	C. Pancreas
_____ 4. Oxytocin	D. Thyroid
_____ 5. Estrogen	E. Ovaries
_____ 6. Growth hormone	F. Parathyroid
_____ 7. Progesterone	G. Pineal
_____ 8. Testosterone	H. Adrenal Cortex
_____ 9. Luteinizing hormone	I. Adrenal Medulla
_____ 10. Insulin	J. Testes
_____ 11. Thyroxin	
_____ 12. Glucagon	
_____ 13. Noradrenalin	
_____ 14. Parathormone	
_____ 15. Prolactin	
_____ 16. Melatonin	
_____ 17. Follicle-stimulating hormone	
_____ 18. Corticotrophin	
_____ 19. Antidiuretic hormone	

Answers to Quiz on Glands and Hormones

1. H
2. I
3. A
4. B
5. E
6. A
7. E
8. J
9. A
10. C
11. D
12. C
13. I
14. F
15. A
16. G
17. A
18. A
19. B

AN OVERVIEW OF GENETICS

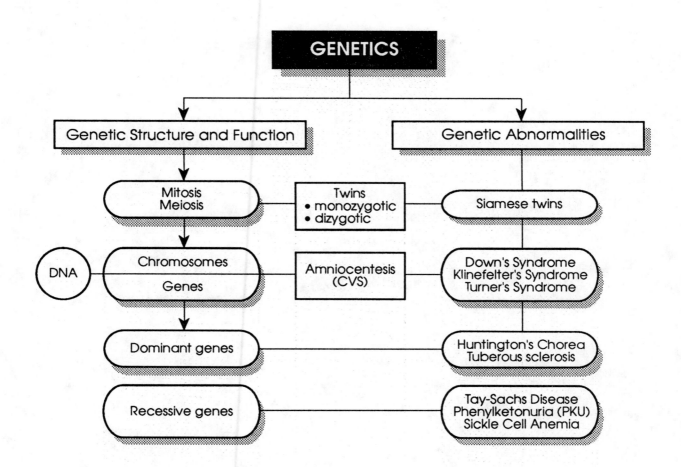

DOMINANT AND RECESSIVE CHARACTERISTICS

Characteristics in the left-hand column (the phenotype) dominate over those characteristics listed in the right-hand column.

	Dominant Traits	Recessive Traits
Eye Coloring	Brown eyes	Grey, green, hazel, blue eyes
	Grey, green, hazel eyes	Blue
	Blue eyes	Albino (pink)
Vision	Farsightedness	Normal vision
	Normal vision	Nearsightedness
	Normal sight	Night vision
	Normal color vision	Color blindness*
Hair	Dark hair	Blonde hair, light hair (red hair)
	Non-red hair (blonde, brunette)	Red hair
	Curly hair	Straight hair
	Full head of hair	Baldness*
	Widow's peak hairline	Normal hairline
Facial Features	Dimples in cheek	No dimples
	Unattached earlobes	Attached earlobes
	"Roman" nose	Straight nose
	Broad lips	Thin lips
Appendages	Extra digits	Normal number
	Fused digits	Normal finger/toes
	Short digits	Normal length
	Fingers lack 1 joint	Normal length
	Limb dwarfing	Normal proportion
	Clubbed thumb	Normal thumb
	Double-jointedness	Normal joints
Other	Immunity to poison ivy	Susceptibility to poison ivy
	Normal coloring (pigmented skin)	Albinism
	Normal blood clotting	Hemophilia*
	Normal hearing	Congenital deafness
	Normal hearing	Deaf mutism
	Normal enzyme profile	Phenylketonuria

Sex-Linked characteristics.

THE SHOCKLEY CASE

Stanley Wellborn

When sociobiologists contend that their work is merely the latest chapter in the Darwinian revolution, they provoke a visceral reaction in many quarters. "One of the more certain ways of insuring a lively and often acrimonious debate is to whisper the word 'sociobiologist' in a crowd of academics," says Brandeis University anthropologist Dr. Neil Gomberg, who followed sociobiology at a discreet distance.

Unable to hold back the swelling tide of evidence for the importance of genes, supporters of the nurture side of the equation have tried to fight back with words. They cite the work of Ivan Pavlov, the famed Soviet psychologist whose salivating dogs inspired his description of the conditioned response, and B.F. Skinner, the Harvard psychologist renowned for his experiments with conditioning of rats and pigeons. Both behaviorists believed that individuals are programed totally by learned responses to the environment.

To call attention to what they see as the dangers of subscribing to genetic destiny, the nurturists lob political grenades. Those who believe in the primacy of genes, observes Harvard biologist Ruth Hubbard, "portray people as biologically adapted to live in competitive, hierarchical societies in which men dominate women and a small, privileged group of men dominates everyone else." That "simplistic and dangerous" philosophy, says Christopher Jencks, a professor at Northwestern University at Evanston, Ill., ignores that crime, poverty, and alienation have social causes too.

Finally, the nurturists raise the specter that the principles of sociobiology are likely to be used irresponsibly by would-be social engineers. The eugenics movement of the 1920's promised to improve the human species through selective breeding — but found a home instead in the horrific death-camp "medical experiments" of Josef Mengele in Germany. Critics of sociobiology hear an ominous echo in recent advances in genetic engineering that can select and enhance certain characteristics. Says Massachusetts Institute of Technology biologist Ethan Signer: "This research is going to bring us one more step closer to genetic engineering of people. That's where they figure out how to have us produce children with ideal characteristics. Last time around, the ideal children had blond hair, blue eyes and Aryan genes."

Such worries aren't just hypothetical. Just three years ago, William Shockley, a Nobel Prize-winning physicist who argues that blacks are genetically inferior in intelligence to whites, took the stand in a $1 million libel suit against the "Atlanta Constitution" to discourse on "dysgenics" — his theory that intelligence is declining because of over-breeding among the "genetically disadvantaged," a category in which he includes most blacks. People of child-bearing age whose IQ's measure below 100 , whose incomes are too low to be taxed and who agree to be sterilized, Shockley proposed, should be paid $1,000 for each IQ point below 100. A column in the newspaper had compared his views to Nazi efforts to wipe out Jews and produce a superhuman race. The jury agreed that Shockley had indeed been libeled but awarded him a token $1 because he'd used the trial as a forum to draw attention to his views.

Singapore, on the other hand, has bought the Shockley doctrine. In this bustling Westernized country, people with less than a university education are rewarded for agreeing to be sterilized after the birth of their first or second child, and parents with degrees are being given incentives to have large numbers of children. Prime Minister Lee Kuan Yew promotes the policy by saying that gradual genetic deterioration will cause Singapore's national "levels of competence" to drop. "Our economy will falter, the administration will suffer and the society will decline," says Lee.

Could Shockley and Lee be right? Do different social classes have distinct genetic traits? Do "upper" classes gradually accumulate a superior gene pool? David Lebedoff, a Minneapolis attorney and author of the 1981 book, *The New Elite,* answers yes to these last two questions. He puts the case for what he terms "biological stratification: bluntly: "People still marry within their social and economic class, but membership in such classes has come to depend more on measurable intelligence and less on circumstances of birth. People of high IQ marry other people of high IQ."

The ingredients that go into intelligence, however, go beyond genes. Intrigued because black youngsters seemed to score lower on standard IQ tests than their white counterparts, psychologist Sandra Scarr of the University of Virginia studied a group of black children raised by white, middle class families. These children's IQ scores averaged 20 points higher than those of the other black children, largely because their home environments were superior. "IQ is a combination of heredity and educational environment," asserts Scarr. "A lot of agony has been fostered because the idea got out that intelligence was inborn and unchangeable."

Technology has given this flawed idea an updated twist. The Repository for Germinal Choice, a sperm bank in California, lures prospective mothers with genes of Nobel Prize winners and other men of high achievement, some no longer living. So far, 39 children have been born with deep-frozen sperm from the repository — but it's too soon to tell whether genetic firepower has produced superior brainpower.

Given that no investigator has demonstrated that any one human being is 100 percent genetically preordained, the nature – nurture equation should be brought into perspective. "A lot of people have the simple-minded notion that a gene turns on and magically blossoms into a behavior," declares Gerald McClearn, a psychologist and twins researcher at Pennsylvania State University. "A gene can produce a nudge in one direction or another, but it does not directly control behavior. It doesn't take away a person's free will." Even E. O. Wilson, the most radical sociobiologist, doesn't believe that behavior goose-steps to the cadence of the genes. "Admitting that we are all influenced in different ways by our genetic coding doesn't reduce our freedom to do what we want to do," he says. The latest research clearly tips the scales toward the nature side — and that's all it does. Researchers agree that people are creatures both of their genetic coding and of their cultural and environmental experience. All scientists are doing is learning the proportions of the recipe.

Discussion Questions

1. Define and discuss the nature – nurture argument.

2. Discuss your reactions to Shockley's position about the intellectual inferiority of blacks to whites.

3. Do you agree or disagree with Shockley and Lee's position that people with low intellectual levels should be discouraged from childbirth and those with higher intellectual levels encouraged?

GENES AND BEHAVIOR: A Twin Legacy

Constance Holden

Biology may not be destiny, but genes apparently have a far greater influence on human behavior than is commonly thought.

Similarities ranging from phobias to hobbies to bodily gestures are being found in pairs of twins separated at birth. Many of these behaviors are "things you would never think of looking at if you were going to study the genetics of behavior," says psychologist Thomas J. Bouchard Jr., director of the Minnesota Center for Twin and Adoption Research at the University of Minnesota.

Bouchard reports that so far, exhaustive psychological tests and questionnaires have been completed with approximately 50 pairs of fraternal twins reared apart and comparison groups of twins reared together.

"We were amazed at the similarity" in posture and expressive style, says Bouchard. "It's probably the feature of the study that's grabbed us the most." Twins tend to have similar mannerisms, gestures, speed and tempo in talking, habits and jokes.

Many of the twins dressed in similar fashion — one male pair who had never previously met arrived in England sporting identical beards, haircuts, wire-rimmed glassed and shirts. (Their photo shows them both with thumbs hooked into their pants tops.) One pair had practically the same items in their toilet cases, including the same brand of cologne and a Swedish brand of toothpaste.

Although many of the separated pairs had differing types of jobs and educational levels, the investigators are finding repeated similarities in hobbies and interests — one pair were both volunteer firefighters, one pair were deputy sheriffs, a male pair had similar workshops in their basements and a female pair had strikingly similar kitchen arrangements.

In one case, two women from different social classes, one of whom was a pharmacological technician and the other a bookkeeper and high school dropout, had results on their vocational-interest tests that were "remarkably similar."

Bouchard doesn't have enough information on abnormal behavior or psychopathology to make generalizations, but he has found repeated similarities. One pair of women were both very superstitious; another pair would burst into tears at the drop of a hat, and questioning revealed that both had done so since childhood. "They were on a talk show together and both started crying in response to one of the questions," says Bouchard. A third pair had the same fears and phobias. Both were afraid of water and had adopted the same coping strategy: backing into the ocean up to their knees. Bouchard took them to a shopping center one day, driving up a long winding parking ramp to let them off. He later learned that they were both so frightened by the drive they sat on a bench for two hours to collect themselves.

The most striking example of common psychopathology, however, came from a pair of fraternal twins, one of whom was reared by his own (poor) family; the other had been adopted into a "good solid upper-middle-class family." Both are now considered to be antisocial personalities, suffering from lack of impulse control, and both have criminal histories. Although fraternal twins share, on average, 50 percent of their genes, Bouchard suggests that the overlap is probably considerably more with this pair.

Another eerie congruence that occurred in the absence of identical genes was observed in the case of two identical- twin women reared apart. Each has a son who has won a statewide mathematics contest, one in Wyoming, one in Texas.

Personality similarities between the identical twins reared apart are almost as pervasive as they are with identical twins reared together, according to the results of a test developed by University of Minnesota psychologist Auke Tellegen. His personality questionnaire contains scales such as "social closeness," "harm avoidance" and "well-being." The researchers were especially surprised to find that "traditionalism" — a trait implying conservatism and respect for authority — can be inherited. In fact, says Bouchard, his and other studies have about 11 personality traits that appear to have significant genetic input.

Overall, the emerging findings of the Minnesota study constitute a powerful rebuttal to those who maintain that environmental influences are the primary shaping forces of personality. The textbooks are going to have to be rewritten, Bouchard predicts.

Discussion Questions

1. Discuss what Bouchard believes to be the primary shaping forces of personality.

2. Do you agree that the findings cited in this article constitute a powerful rebuttal to those who maintain that environmental influences are the primary shaping forces of personality? Why?

Chapter 3
Sensation and Perception

AN OVERVIEW OF SENSATION AND PERCEPTION

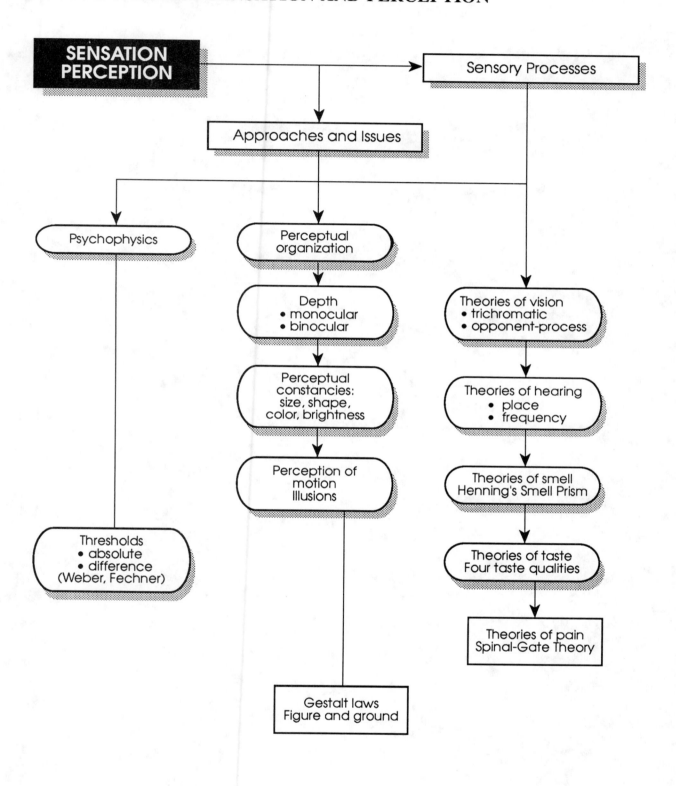

AN OVERVIEW OF SENSORY PROCESSES

Receptors/Sensory Processes	Transducers	Neural Activity

Optic Mechanism	Retina
	  -rod
	  -cones
		Visual acuity
		Color blindness
		Lateral inhibition

Auditory Mechanism	Organ of Corti	Pitch and loudness
		  location
		  hearing loss

Olfactory Mechanism	Olfactory epithelium	Pheromones Menstrual synchrony
Gustatory Mechanism	Taste cells Taste buds	Taste blindness Taste aversion
Cutaneous Mechanism	Skin receptors Free nerve endings and more	Paradoxical cold Relative temperature
Kinesthetic Mechanism	Joints, tendons muscles	Internal feedback Tabes dorsalis
Vestibular Mechanism	Semicircular canals	Motion Sickness Vertigo Centrifugal force
Pain Mechanism	All receptor systems	Referred pain Chronic pain Acute pain

THE HUMAN EYE

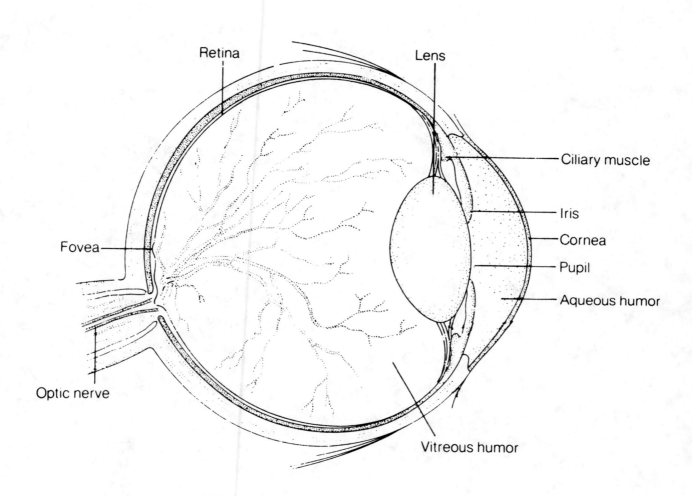

Retina

Lens

Ciliary muscle

Iris

Cornea

Pupil

Aqueous humor

Fovea

Optic nerve

Vitreous humor

VISUAL ILLUSIONS

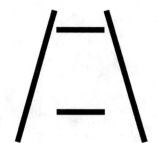

The Ponzo Illusion

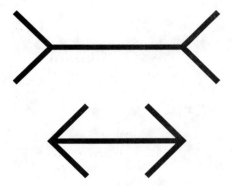

The Müller-Lyer Illusion

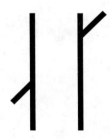

The Poggendorf Illusion

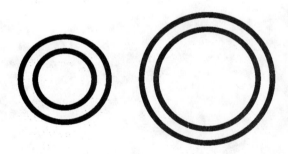

The Delboeuf Illusion

GESTALT PRINCIPLES OF ORGANIZATION

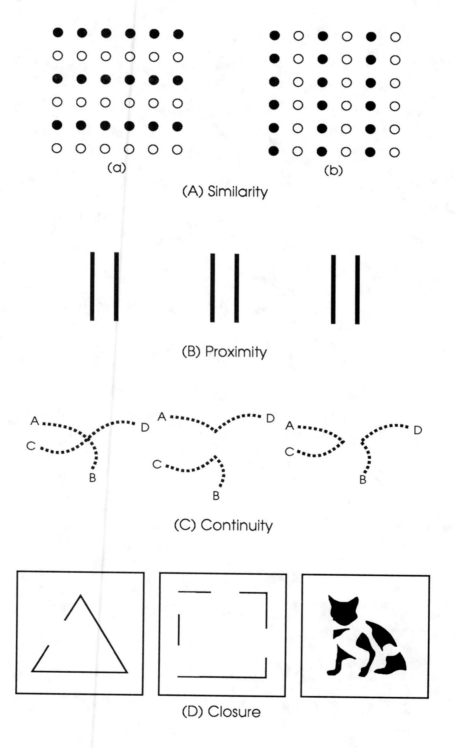

(A) Similarity

(B) Proximity

(C) Continuity

(D) Closure

REVERSIBLE FIGURE – GROUND PATTERNS

What do you see in these two reversible patterns? Is Figure A a picture of two faces or a vase? Is the woman in Figure B young or old?

Figure A

Figure B

THE HUMAN EAR

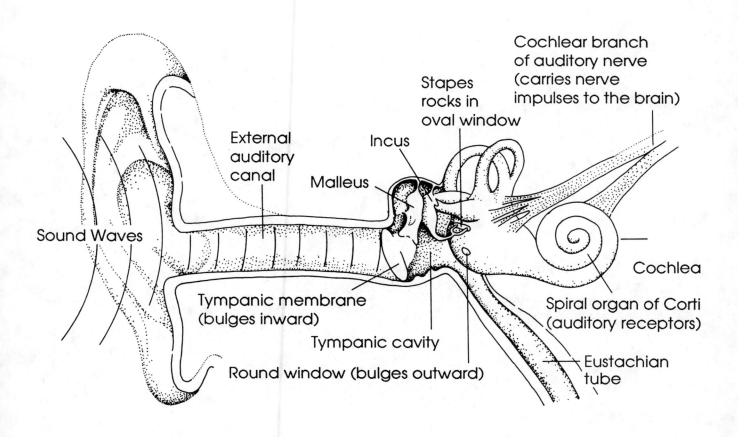

Cochlear branch
of auditory nerve
(carries nerve
impulses to the brain)

Stapes
rocks in
oval window

Incus

External
auditory
canal

Malleus

Sound Waves

Cochlea

Tympanic membrane
(bulges inward)

Spiral organ of Corti
(auditory receptors)

Tympanic cavity

Eustachian
tube

Round window (bulges outward)

EXTERNAL EAR
(air conduction)

MIDDLE EAR
(bone conduction)

INNER EAR
(fluid conduction)

ORGAN OF THE CORTI

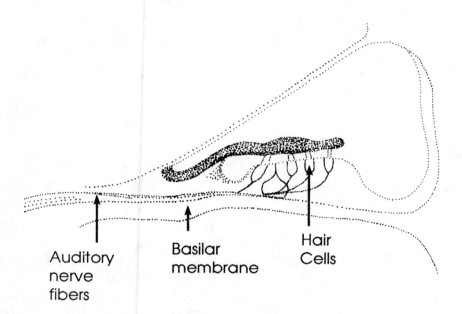

Auditory
nerve
fibers

Basilar
membrane

Hair
Cells

THE TASTE RECEPTORS

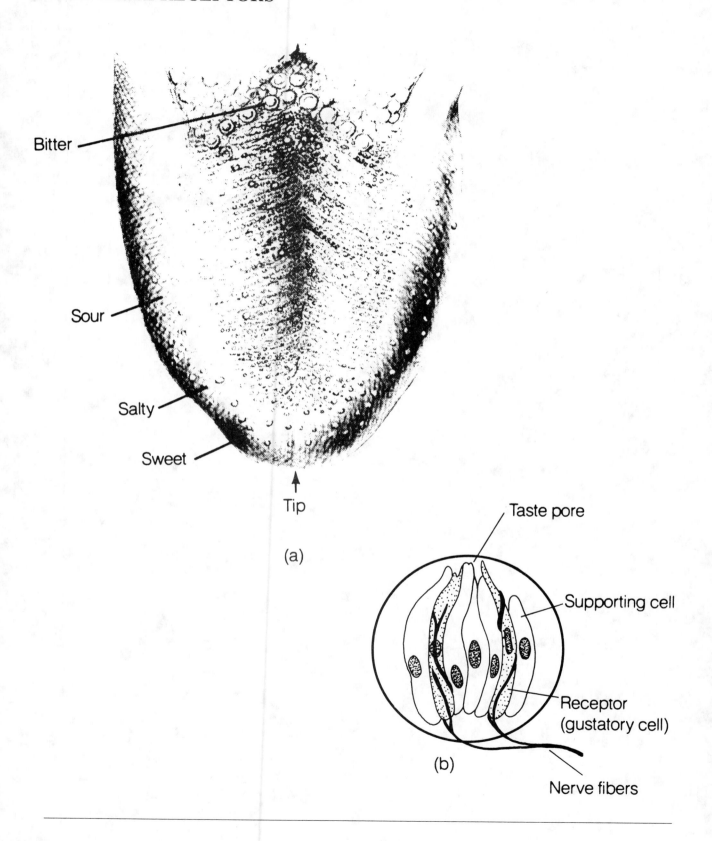

Bitter

Sour

Salty

Sweet

Tip

(a)

Taste pore

Supporting cell

Receptor
(gustatory cell)

(b)

Nerve fibers

THE OLFACTION RECEPTORS

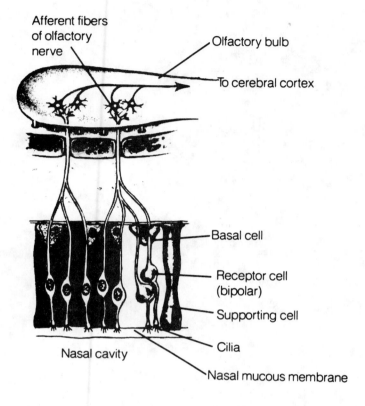

Afferent fibers of olfactory nerve

Olfactory bulb

To cerebral cortex

Basal cell

Receptor cell (bipolar)

Supporting cell

Cilia

Nasal cavity

Nasal mucous membrane

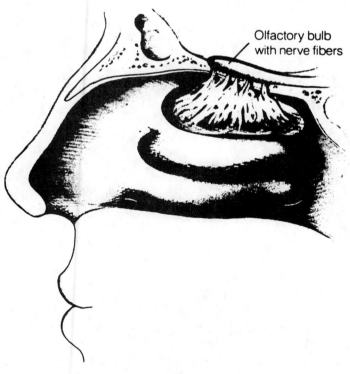

Olfactory bulb with nerve fibers

RECEPTORS FOR THE SKIN SENSES

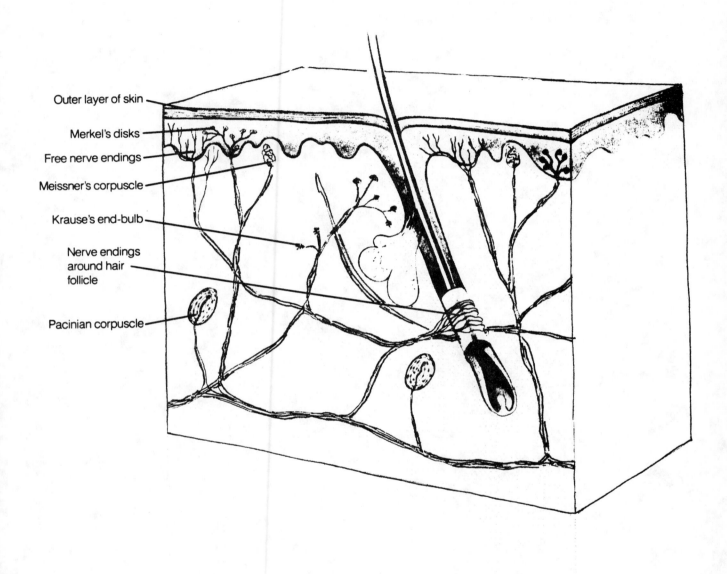

Outer layer of skin

Merkel's disks

Free nerve endings

Meissner's corpuscle

Krause's end-bulb

Nerve endings around hair follicle

Pacinian corpuscle

THE PRESIDENT'S SPEECH

Oliver Sacks

What was going on? A roar of laughter from the aphasia ward, just as the President's speech as starting, and the patients had all been so eager to hear the President speak.

There he was, the old charmer, the actor with his practiced rhetoric, his histrionics, his emotional appeal — and all the patients were convulsed with laughter. Well, not all: some looked bewildered, some looked outraged, one or two looked apprehensive, but most looked amused. The President is generally thought to be a moving speaker — but he was moving them, apparently, mainly to laughter. What could they be thinking? Were they failing to understand him? Or did they, perhaps, understand all too well?

It was often said of these patients, who though intelligent had the severest receptive aphasia, rendering them incapable of understanding words as such, that they nonetheless understood most of what was said to them. Their friends, their relatives, the nurses who knew them well, could hardly believe, sometimes, that they were aphasic. This was because, when addressed naturally, they grasped some or most of the meaning. And one does speak "naturally," naturally.

Thus to demonstrate their aphasia, one had to go to extraordinary lengths, as a neurologist, to speak and behave unnaturally, to remove all the extraverbal cuesv — tone of voice intonation, suggestive emphasis or inflection, as well as all visual cues (one's expressions, one's gestures, one's entire, largely unconscious, personal repertoire and posture). One had to remove all of this (which might involve total concealment of one's person and total depersonalization of one's voice, even to use a computerized voice synthesizer) in order to reduce speech to pure words, speech totally devoid of what Frege called "tone-color" or "evocation." With the most sensitive patients, it was only with such a grossly artificial, mechanical speech, somewhat like that of the computers in Star Trek, that one could be wholly sure of their aphasia.

Why? Because speech — natural speech — does not consist of words alone, or (as the English neurologist Hughlings Jackson thought) of "propositions" alone. It consists of utterance — an uttering forth of one's whole meaning with one's whole being — the understanding of which involves infinitely more than mere word recognition. This was the clue to aphasiacs' understanding, even when they might be wholly uncomprehending of words as such. For though the words, the verbal constructions, per se, might convey nothing, spoken language is normally suffused with "tone," embedded in an expressiveness that transcends the verbal. It is precisely this expressiveness, so deep, so various, so complex, so subtle, that is perfectly reserved in aphasia, though understanding of words be destroyed. Preserved and often more: preternaturally enhanced.

This too becomes clear, often in the most striking or comic or dramatic way, to all those who work or live closely with aphasiacs: their families or friends or nurses or doctors. At first, perhaps, we see nothing much the matter; and then we see that there has been a great change, almost an inversion, in their understanding of speech. Something has gone, been devastated, it is true — but something has come in its stead, has been immensely enhanced, so that, at least with emotionally laden utterance, the meaning may be fully grasped even when every word is missed. This, in our species, seems almost an inversion, and perhaps a reversion too, to something more primitive and elemental. And this perhaps is why Hughlings Jackson compared aphasiacs to dogs (a comparison that might outrage both), though when he did this he was chiefly thinking of their remarkable and almost infallible sensitivity to "tone" and feeling. Henry Head, more sensitive in this regard, speaks of "feeling-tone" in his treatise *Aphasia* (1926), and stresses how it is preserved, and often enhanced, in aphasiacs.

Thus the feeling I sometimes have — which all of us who work closely with aphasiacs have— that one cannot lie to an aphasiac. He cannot grasp your words, and so cannot be deceived by them; but what he grasps he grasps with infallible precision, namely the expression that goes with words, that total, spontaneous, involuntary expressiveness which can never be simulated or faked, as words alone can, all too easily.

We recognize this with dogs, and often use them for this purpose — to pick up falsehood, or malice, or equivocal intentions, to tell us who can be trusted, who is integral, who makes sense — when we, so susceptible to words, cannot trust our own instincts.

And what dogs can do here, aphasiacs do too, and at a human and immeasurably superior level. "One can lie with the mouth," Nietzsche writes, "but with the accompanying grimace one nevertheless tells the truth." To such a grimace, to any falsity or impropriety in bodily appearance or posture, aphasiacs are preternaturally sensitive. And if they cannot see one — this is especially true of our blind aphasiacs — they have an infallible ear for every vocal nuance, the tone, the rhythm, the cadences, the music, the subtlest modulations, inflections, intonations, which can give, or remove, verisimilitude from a man's voice.

In this, then, lies their power of understanding — understanding, without words, what is authentic or inauthentic. Thus it was the grimaces, the histrionisms, the gestures — and, above all, the tones and cadences of the President's voice — that range false for these wordless but immensely sensitive patients. It was to these (for them) most glaring, even grotesque, incongruities and improprieties that my aphasiac patients responded, undeceived and undeceivable by words.

This is why they laughed at the President's speech.

If one cannot lie to an aphasiac, in view of his special sensitivity to expression and "tone", how is it, we might ask, with patients — if there are such — who lack any sense of expression and "tone," while preserving, unchanged, their comprehension for words: patients of an exactly opposite kind? We have a number of such patients, also on the aphasia ward, although technically they do not have aphasia but, instead, a form of agnosia, in particular a so-called tonal agnosia. For such patients, typically, the depressive qualities of voices disappear — their tone, their timbre, their feeling, their entire character — while words (and grammatical constructions) are perfectly understood. Such tonal agnosias (or "atonias") are associated with disorders of the right temporal lobe of the brain, whereas the aphasias go with disorders of the left temporal lobe.

Among the patients with tonal agnosia on our aphasia ward who also listened to the President's speech as Edith D., with a glioma in her right temporal lobe. A former

English teacher and poet of some repute, with an exceptional feeling for language, and strong powers of analysis and expression, Edith was able to articulate the opposite situation — how the President's speech sounded to someone with tonal agnosia. Edith could no longer tell if a voice was angry, cheerful, sad — whatever. Since voices now lacked expression, she had to look at people's faces, their postures and movements when they talked, and found herself doing so with a care, an intensity I had never seen her do before. But this, it so happened, was also limited, because she had a malignant glaucoma and was rapidly losing her sight.

What she then found she had to do was to pay extreme attention to the exactness of words and word use, and to insist that those around her did just the same. She could less and less follow loose speech or slang — speech of an allusive or emotional kind — and more and more required of her interlocutors that they speak prose, "proper words in proper places." Prose might, she found, compensate, in some degree, for lack of perceived tone or feeling.

In this way she was able to preserve, even enhance, the use of "expressive" speech (to use Frege's distinction), in which meaning is largely given by the apt choice and reference of words, despite being more and more lost with "evocative" speech, where meaning is largely given in the use and sense of tone.

Edith also listened, stony-faced, to the President's speech, bringing to it a strange mixture of enhanced and defective perceptions — precisely the opposite mixture from those of our aphasiacs. It did not move her — no speech now moved her — and all that was evocative, genuine or false, completely passed her by. Deprived of emotional reaction, was she then transported or taken in? By no means. "He is not cogent," she said. "He does not speak good prose. His word use is improper. Either he is brain-damaged, or he has something to conceal." Thus, the President's speech did not work for Edith either, owing to her enhanced sense of formal language use, propriety as prose, any more than it worked for our aphasiacs, with their word-deafness but enhanced sense of tone.

Here then was the paradoxical possibility raised by the President's speech. That a good many normal people, aided, doubtless, by their wish to be fooled, were indeed well and truly fooled. And so cunningly was deceptive word use combined with deceptive tone, that it was the brain-damaged who remained undeceived.

Discussion Questions

1. Distinguish between aphasia and agnosia.

2. Try this simple exercise. Turn the volume completely off on your television set. By watching the facial movements, hand gestures, and postures of the speakers, were you able to sense their emotional states? the truthfulness of their words? Compare and contrast your experiences with the experiences of others.

PHENOMENA, COMMENT AND NOTES

Michael H. Robinson

Heads of museums and zoos can learn a lot by eavesdropping. As director of the National Zoo in Washington, I find that "listening in" is a corrective for my unalloyed enthusiasms; not everybody thinks that animals are beautiful or exciting. I hear preferences and aversions that are foreign to my outlook. One recurring revelation is that people in general think of animals as rather strange humans. Identifying animals with humans is totally regrettable. We urgently need to increase concern for the welfare of animals, both as species and as individuals, but to do this we need to appreciate that in most cases they live very different lives in a very different world. I think that zoos have reinforced people's tendencies to anthropomorphize animals. We have done this through the nature of our exhibits.

In presenting animals in natural settings, zoos have made enormous strides in recent years. They have moved from art gallery displays of isolated animals — masterpieces — to balanced social groupings of species, and from sterilizable cages — tiled like bathrooms — to naturalistic habitats. The word "cage" is no longer a valid or accurate description of most animal habitats in modern zoos.

Unfortunately, in making these great advances we have continued to be strikingly homocentric. We present our habitat exhibits to human scale, from a human focal length, from human eye level, and literally colored by the biases of our sense organs. This is unfortunate because modern studies of animal behavior show that most animals not only have a different picture of the world but also attend to different parts of it. (Notice the emphasis on vision in our language and our figures of speech.) Many animals smell the world rather than see it, and many that do see it, see it in black and white, or myopically, or microscopically.

Thus it is worth thinking about some exhibits that could show us the animals' world. For example, squirrels and their relatives — the gophers, chipmunks and prairie dogs — have a very different color vision from our own. Because of the structure of their retinas we know that they are most likely red-green color-blind. The green grasses of the prairies are not green to the prairie dog. We could easily make an exhibit that was an accurate representation of the prairie dog's world. Even the New World monkeys have a different color sense. The world of the deer might seem stranger yet. Most of the time, deer probably do not see color at all. To illustrate this point, we could set up some mannequins near the deer yard, one dressed in traditional bright-colored hunter's garb and the other in black and white. We could explain that the deer probably sees both as black and white — the color of the hunting jacket is only to alert other hunters.

We all know from our own experience how predators see; their eyes are on the front of their heads, which ensures stereoscopic vision and good depth perception. But we don't know what it is like to see laterally like most prey animals. The British Museum (Natural History) in London has an exhibit that makes a striking point about lateral vision. Rearview car mirrors are mounted so that when you look in them you have a rabbit's eye view of the world. The rabbit sees to the side and to the rear, though not very well to the front, and it has a much wider field of view than ours.

It is worth considering how we might operate if we had such wide-screen vision. As it is, we tend to concentrate our attention at the centerpoint of our gaze and filter out and ignore many peripheral objects. (Just think of the behavior of the other drivers that you encounter in the average day!) What would happen if we had a nearly 360-degree field of view? Ever since I saw the London exhibit, I've been thinking about designing a device that would demonstrate how a rabbit sees. First, it would completely block frontal vision while providing 120-degree lateral and rear vision. Then, it would need a visor and cunningly mounted prisms. Such spectacles would turn a child's vision into that of a color conscious rabbit. Even better would be movable ears connected to earphones to illustrate the rabbit's directional hearing. (When I was a schoolteacher I often longed for the ears of a rabbit!)

So far we have discussed only spectral sensitivity and angle of view. If we include scale and focus, things get more complex. In my late maturity — old age — I see most close objects in a blur whenever I have lost my eyeglasses. Some animals spend their entire lives in such a blur, seeing only distant objects clearly. Other animals see little farther than our arm's length. Perhaps we should design an exhibit to illustrate this too.

Discussion Questions

1. Given that the author is correct in his assessment, how should zoos or animal habitats be designed? Give several examples of the type of changes that should be made.

2. What potential long-term effects might these changes have on the animal kingdom, particularly species that are on the endangered lists?

3. Compare and contrast human perception with that of a rabbit, a prairie dog, a deer, and a chipmunk.

Chapter 4
States of Consciousness

SLEEP: APPROACHES AND ISSUES

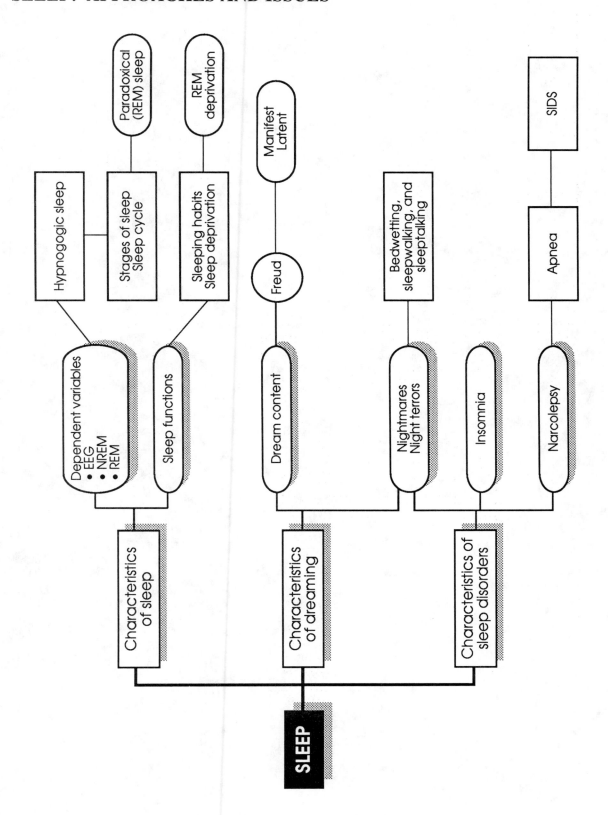

AN OVERVIEW OF DRUG-RELATED BEHAVIORS

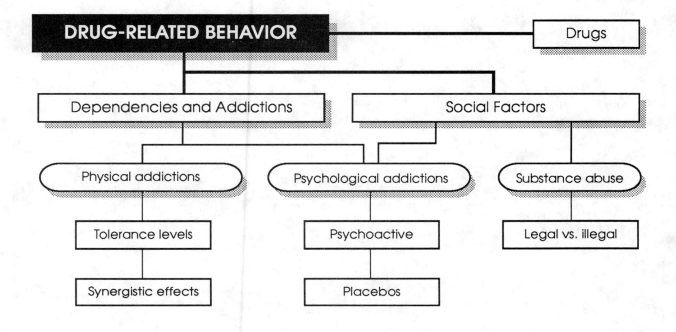

AN OVERVIEW OF DRUGS

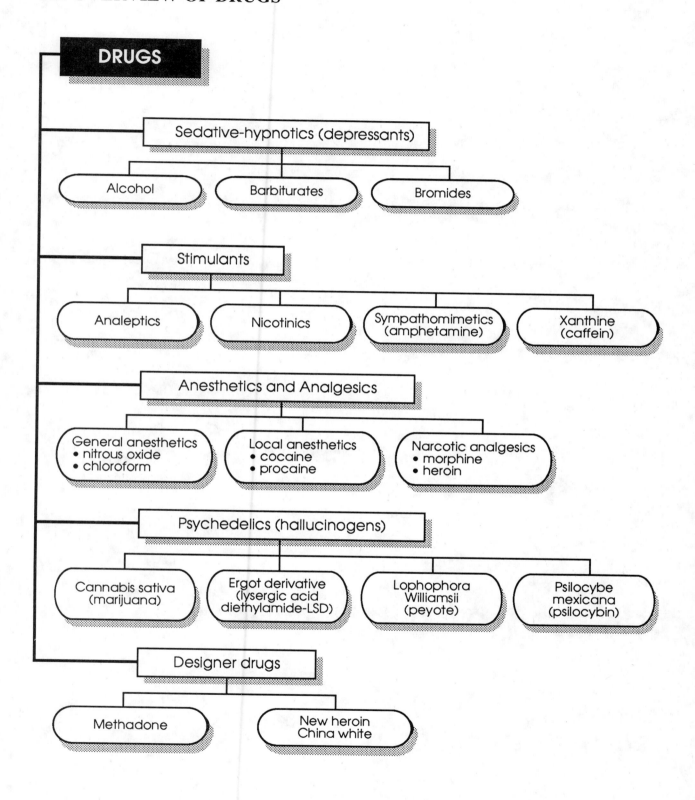

DRUGS

Sedative-hypnotics (depressants)
- Alcohol
- Barbiturates
- Bromides

Stimulants
- Analeptics
- Nicotinics
- Sympathomimetics (amphetamine)
- Xanthine (caffein)

Anesthetics and Analgesics
- General anesthetics
  - nitrous oxide
  - chloroform
- Local anesthetics
  - cocaine
  - procaine
- Narcotic analgesics
  - morphine
  - heroin

Psychedelics (hallucinogens)
- Cannabis sativa (marijuana)
- Ergot derivative (lysergic acid diethylamide-LSD)
- Lophophora Williamsii (peyote)
- Psilocybe mexicana (psilocybin)

Designer drugs
- Methadone
- New heroin China white

SUMMARY CHART OF DRUGS AND THEIR EFFECTS

Category	Drugs	Sample Trade or Other Names	Medical Uses	Physical Addiction	Psychological Addiction	Possible Effects
Cannabis	Marijuana	Pot, grass, reefer, sinsemilla	Experimental and research only	Moderate with heavy use	Moderate	Euphoria, relaxed inhibitions, increase in heart and pulse rate, reddening of the eyes, increased appetite, disoriented behavior.
	Tetrahydrocannabinol	THC				
	Hashish	Hash				
	Hash Oil	Hash Oil				
Depressants	Alcohol	Liquor, wine, beer	None	High	High	Slurred speech, disorientation, drunken behavior
	Barbiturates	Secobarbital, Amobarbital, Butisol, Tuinal	Anesthetic, anti-convulsant sedative, hypnotic	High–Moderate	High–Moderate	
	Methaqualone	Quaalude, Sopor, Parest	Sedative hypnotic	High	High	
	Tranquilizers	Valium, Librium, Equanil, Miltown	Anti-anxiety Anti-convulsant sedative	Moderate–Low	Moderate	

Category	Drugs	Sample Trade or Other Names	Medical Uses	Physical Addiction	Psychological Addiction	Possible Effects
Stimulants	Cocaine	Coke, flake, snow, girl	Local anesthetic	Low	High	Increased alertness, excitation, euphoria, increase in pulse rate and blood pressure, insomnia, loss of appetite.
	Crack			Low		
	Amphetamines	Dexedrine Biphetamine	Hyperactivity, narcolepsy			
	Nicotine	Tobacco, cigars, cigarettes	Emetic	Moderate	High	
	Caffeine	Coffee, tea, cola drinks, No-Doz	Part of some over-the-counter medication	Low	Moderate	
Hallucinogens	LSD	Acid	Research only	Low	Degree unknown	Illusions and hallucinations, poor perception of time and distance.
	Mescaline & Peyote	Button, cactus	None			
	Phencyclidine	PCP, angel dust	Veterinary anesthetic	Low	High	
	Psilocybin, psilocin	Mushrooms	None	None	Degree unknown	

Category	Drugs	Sample Trade or Other Names	Medical Uses	Physical Addiction	Psychological Addiction	Possible Effects
Inhalants	Nitrous oxide	Whippets, laughing gas	Anesthetic	Possible	Moderate	Excitement, euphoria, giddiness, loss of inhibition, aggressiveness, drowsiness, headache.
	Butyl nitrite	Locker room	None			
	Amyl nitrite	Poppers, snappers	Heart stimulant			
	Chlorohydro-carbons	Aerosal paint, cleaning fluid	None			
	Hydrocarbons	Aerosal propellants, gasoline, glue, paint thinner	None			
Narcotics	Opium	Paregoric	Antidiarrheal, pain relief	High	High	Euphoria, drowsiness, respiratory depression, constricted pupils, nausea.
	Morphine	Morphine, pectoral syrup				
	Codeine	Codeine, Empirin compound with codeine, Robitussin A–C		Moderate	Moderate	
	Heroin	Horse, smack, boy	Under investigation	High	High	
	Methadone	Dolophine, Methadose	Heroin substitute, pain relief			

QUIZ: HOW MUCH DO YOU KNOW ABOUT CRACK AND COCAINE?

True or False

_____ 1. Cocaine is a psychoactive drug that is obtained from the South American cocoa bush.

_____ 2. Cocaine is reported to be the largest producer of illicit income of all drugs in the United States.

_____ 3. Dr. Sigmund Freud once recommended the use of cocaine in the treatment of both nervousness and morphine addiction.

_____ 4. In 1988, Dr. J. C. Pemberton introduced a drink containing cocaine and called it Dr. Pepper.

_____ 5. The Harrison Narcotic Act of 1914 made it legal to use cocaine for non-medical purposes.

_____ 6. Crack cocaine is used intravenously.

_____ 7. Crack cocaine is sold in a pure "rock" form.

_____ 8. Since crack is similar to free base cocaine, it is pure and cannot damage the body.

_____ 9. Crack has been associated with heart problems in users.

_____ 10. Cocaine (crack) can be detected in body fluids for about a week after use.

_____ 11. Cocaine use in any form (crack) can cause addiction.

Multiple Choice

12. The euphoria produced by crack generally lasts

   (a) 60 minutes
   (b) 45 minutes
   (c) 30 minutes
   (d) 5 minutes

13. The euphoria produced by powdered cocaine lasts about

   (a) 60 minutes
   (b) 45 minutes
   (c) 30 minutes
   (d) 15 minutes

14. Cocaine or crack use causes

   (a) insomnia
   (b) weight loss
   (c) chronic fatigue
   (d) all of the above

15. Cocaine or crack can cause

   (a) seizures
   (b) heart attacks
   (c) irregular heartbeats
   (d) all of the above

Quiz on Cocaine Answers

1. T
2. T
3. T
4. F
5. F
6. F
7. F
8. F
9. T
10. T
11. T
12. D
13. B
14. D
15. D

THE STUFF OF DREAMS

The biblical Joseph who interpreted Pharaoh's dream of seven fat and seven lean kine, though one of the best known, was by no means the first to find signs of the future in dreams. People in most known civilizations have accorded dreams a supernatural origin. They were often regarded as messages from gods or spirits.

In the modern world dreams are usually regarded as messages from oneself. The most influential twentieth-century theory is Freud's. He held that the "latent" content of a dream — which is uncovered largely by the intricate technique of free association of ideas — is usually a form of wish-fulfilment. Dreams mostly reflect infantile sexuality.

Later theories of dreams, especially in America, have moved on from Freud in four ways.

- They reject the idea that dreams are mostly hidden wishes. Instead, dreams might reflect almost any kind of emotion.

- When they do signify wishes, these need not derive from childhood eroticism. A dreamer might wish anything.

- Free association is not particularly important for understanding dreams. Indeed, the two sit oddly together. If free-association can be a route to the unconscious, applying it to dreams looks like overkill. Why not free-associate on the subject of a postage stamp instead?

- Freud's idea that a dream's meaning is buried deep beneath its apparent content is losing favour. Many analysts, influenced by Carl Jung, try to "amplify" the apparent content of a dream to find some significance. They think that dreams reveal, rather than conceal.

Dr. David Foulkes at Emory University in Atlanta, Georgia, has developed a theory of dreams that is Freudian in inspiration but takes most of these criticisms into account. Like Freud, he thinks that dreams are at least as complex as conscious thoughts, and just as worthwhile to study. He notes that it is easy to get long detailed reports of the contents of dreams.

Dr. Foulkes's account of dream-reports uses the semi-mathematical tools developed for the analysis of language by Dr. Noam Chomsky. Freud himself would hardly recognize it. But this would not surprise Rabbi Bizna. In the Babylonian Talmud, which contains rabbinical commentaries from the first millennium BC, Rabbi Bizna recounts that he was given 24 different interpretations of the same dream, all of which were correct. Many post-Freudians agree that each dream has many meanings.

The results of physiology are more definite. At some time during a night's sleep, a sleeper's eyes start moving under his closed lids. If he is woken up during this "rapid eye movement" sleep, he will almost invariably say that he was dreaming.

Another way to tell whether something is going on in a sleeping mind is to use an electroencephalogram (EEG). This measures electrical activity in the brain — that is, brainwaves. EEGs reveal three types of sleep with different characteristic brainwave patterns: light sleep, deep sleep and active sleep. Light sleep and deep sleep are typified by slow, simple waves.

In active sleep, the sleeper's brainwave patterns are very like those of a person who is awake. This sleep takes place at the same time as the rapid eye movements and is sometimes called REM sleep. Other features of active sleep include an increased flow of blood especially to the brain and the genitals, and a sort of temporary paralysis. Breathing and heartbeat become irregular.

Active sleep takes place for periods of around 20 minutes every 90 minutes or so during sleep. In all, around a quarter of the night is spent in active sleep. If sleep continues well into the morning, the mind slides in and out of waking and dreaming. Dreams had during this phase are the ones most often remembered.

Not only people dream. Nearly all the mammals studies so far show signs of REM in sleep. Birds, too, seem to have different kinds of sleep. How this sleep is arranged depends on what sort of environment the animal lives in. Animals which live amid danger sleep in short bursts.

Active sleep and dreaming are not exactly the same thing. People woken up from deep sleep will often be able to answer the question, "what was going through your mind?" So there is some activity in the brain during deep sleep. But the thought found in deep sleep is prosaic.

What is going on when somebody dreams? One theory is that the brain is freewheeling. Descriptions of dreams are similar to descriptions of illusions had during sensory deprivation. When somebody is enclosed in a dark, silent place for long enough, he will hallucinate. Dreams may be the normal activity of the brain when it is deprived of sensations.

But not every dream is freewheeling. Between 5-10% of people have what are known as lucid dreams — that is dreams that are under their control. Most people have an inkling of this at its simplest: the sensation that a dream is just a dream.

Dr. Steven LaBerge, at the Sleep Research Centre at Stanford University in California, has communicated with sleeping people while they are dreaming lucidly. In one experiment he investigated the passage of time. His subjects agreed to count to ten during their reveries . When they reached each number they would signal by moving their eyes. Each number was to represent one second of dream time.

Dr. LaBerge found that dreamers estimates of dream time are roughly as accurate as wakers' estimate of waking time. But dream time is not tied to real time. In a dream, as in a film, the boring bits are often skipped.

There is a telling difference between waking thought and sleeping thought. In dreams, the body is disconnected from the mind. The brain gets little information from the rest of the body and the body cannot hear the orders the brain sends out. When you dream of doing something, your body does not go through the motions of actually doing it.

A part of the brain inhibits most of the body's muscular actions during active sleep — apart from breathing, eye movements, and a few other things. Such "sleep paralysis" sometimes carries on for a few seconds into wakefulness. You wake up from a dream and cannot move.

In the 1960s, Dr. Michael Jouvet shed some light on sleep paralysis. Cats that have had cuts made deep in their brains do odd things while asleep. They perform complex actions, show anger, fear, and other emotions. Dr. Jouvet surmised that surgery damaged a part of the cats' brains that normally switched off the body during dreaming.

Some people, too, act out their dreams. Most often they are older men. It is rare in young ones and almost unheard of in women. It is not like everyday sleep-walking or sleep-talking, both of which happen during deep sleep. The movements are not slow, repetitive or automatic, like those of a sleep walker. They are quick and complex. Most of those who suffer from it have had neurological problems. A drug called clonazepam, a relative of a tranquilizer, Valium, appears to stop the body from paying attention to dream.

When people dream and what they dream are fairly well known. How and why they dream is less clear. How, for example, does dreaming start? Dr. Allan Hobson at Harvard Medical School suggests a way to explain the switch between deep sleep and active sleep. It sheds some light on dreaming. He argues that sleep is controlled by an oscillating system that swings from one state to another — rather like a pendulum, except that the oscillations in the brain are chemical, not mechanical.

Most descriptions of the brain compare it to a computer. True, cells communicate electrically. But there are tiny gaps between the ends of the "wires" that the cell use to communicate. These gaps are bridged by chemicals. Such a system is flexible: an electrical current can only be on or off; but different chemicals can be released to give different sorts of message, and each chemical can vary in concentration.

Dr. Hobson found groups of cells in the brain stem (the part of the brain between the spinal cord and the cortex) which seem to oscillate during sleep in just the right way. Some of the cells have wires which release a chemical called noradrenaline. Others nearby release acetylcholine.

Acetylcholine and noradrenaline act on cells in different ways. Acetylcholine makes cells respond to arriving information more enthusiastically; noradrenaline calms the cells down and makes them more selective. When people are awake, both groups of cells work together. They have connections all around the brain, so they are useful for providing a beat that synchronizes different parts of the brain. They are like a metronome sending out pulsing levels of their chemicals.

In sleep things change. In deep sleep, small amounts of both chemicals circulate, which explains the brain's quiescence. During deep sleep the level of noradrenaline is falling and the level of acetylcholine slowly rising. Once a certain threshold is crossed, something dramatic happens. Levels of noradrenaline plummet while lots of acetylcholine is released. The brain has moved into active sleep.

During active sleep, levels of acetylcholine decline. When the threshold is crossed, they suddenly fall and those of noradrenaline rise. This takes the sleep cycle back to the its beginning. It is at this point that a sleeper is most likely to wake up.

Changing levels of acetylcholine and noradrenaline help explain dreaming. A stimulus, such as "elephant", fed to a brain bathed in acetycholine would spontaneously produce thoughts such as "Dumbo, Mickey Mouse, cheese, photography,

Byzantine icon." That is, plenty of bizarre associations — just as in dreams. Noradrenaline forestalls such associations. It probably has a role in helping concentration during wakefulness.

Noradrenaline is involved in memory. Most theories say that long-term memory requires protein synthesis, which noradrenaline helps. Without the links provided by noradrenaline, what happens during active sleep will probably not be remembered. For the most part, dreams will fade before morning.

Why does the brain need this night-time activity? One answer is that it runs out of chemicals during the day and needs to replenish its stocks at night. People starved of active sleep start to lost their concentration and may hallucinate. Rats deprived of sleep die from loss of appetite and being unable to control their body temperature. It all looks like a lack of noradrenaline.

Dr. Hobson's account of how people dream may explain why they dream. One theory is that dreaming lets memories get stored away correctly. The brain takes in huge amounts of information during the day, only some of which needs to be remembered. Perhaps the point of dreams is, as Freud once suggested, to help forget.

One theory of memory has it that when something new is learned, new connections are made in a network of brain cells. Some of these connections will be faulty; the brain needs to sort out which they are. To do this, the network has to be put through its paces so that bad connections can be found and "unlearned".

The first unlearning theory was first put forward in this form by Dr. Francis Crick and Dr. Graeme Mitchison, both then at Cambridge University, in 1983. It has serious problems, as do all theories of dreaming. But it might provide an explanation for one puzzle about anteaters.

The echidna, a spiny anteater found in Australia, has an extraordinarily large cortex. It is also a mammal — albeit a very primitive one — which does not show any signs of REM sleep. Theory suggests that if there is no way to correct a faulty memory, a good alternative might be to make the network bigger. That appears to be what the spiny anteater does.

The forgetting theory is one of many. Some hold that dreams are meaningless side-effects of the brain's housekeeping. Others that they are a way of coping with emotional problems. Another theory holds that dreams are dry-runs that test circuits before they are needed. This fits neatly with the fact that fetuses spend almost all their time-in active sleep.

The newest suggestion comes from Dr. Thomas Wehr at the Institute of Mental Health in Bethesda, Maryland. He thinks that animals sleep to conserve energy when it is dark. Sleeping animals get cold and a cold brain is hard to switch on. In a hostile environment, that makes animals vulnerable. Dreaming is a way of heating up the brain, like revving a car, so that it is ready for action.

Discussion Questions

1. List and compare the different stages of sleep.

2. Compare and contrast at least three theories of dreaming.

3. What role(s) do noradrenaline and acetylcholine play in dreams?

Chapter 5
Learning

AN OVERVIEW OF LEARNING

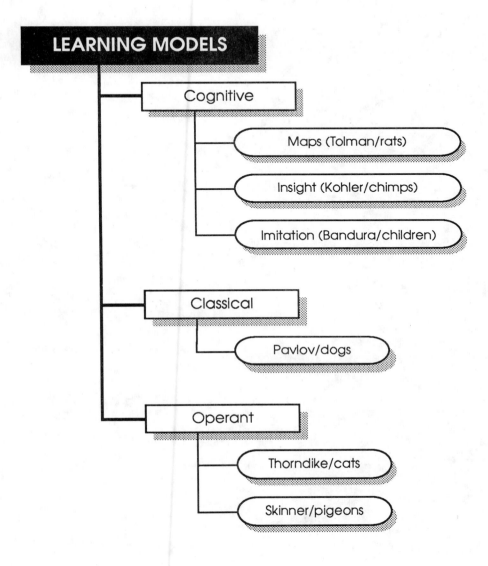

AN OVERVIEW OF CLASSICAL CONDITIONING

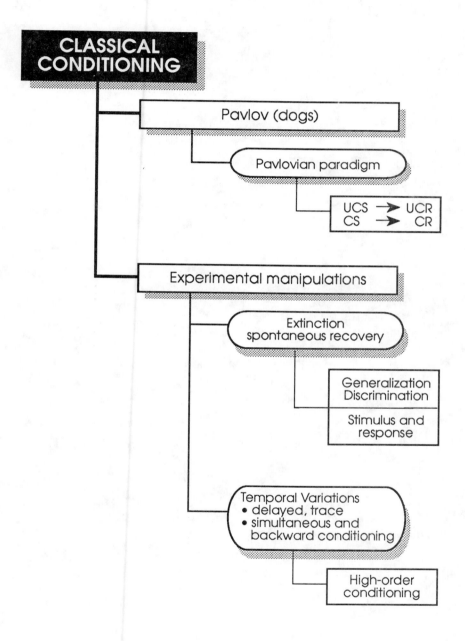

AN OVERVIEW OF OPERANT CONDITIONING

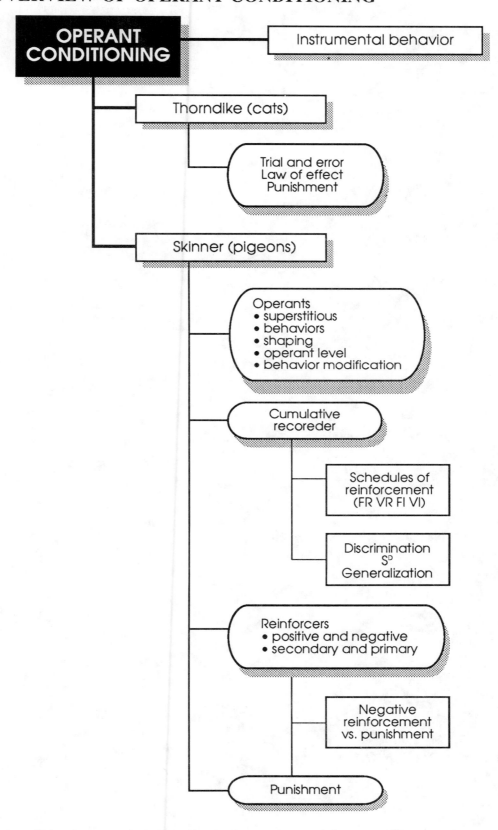

THE EFFECTS OF REINFORCERS AND PUNISHMENT

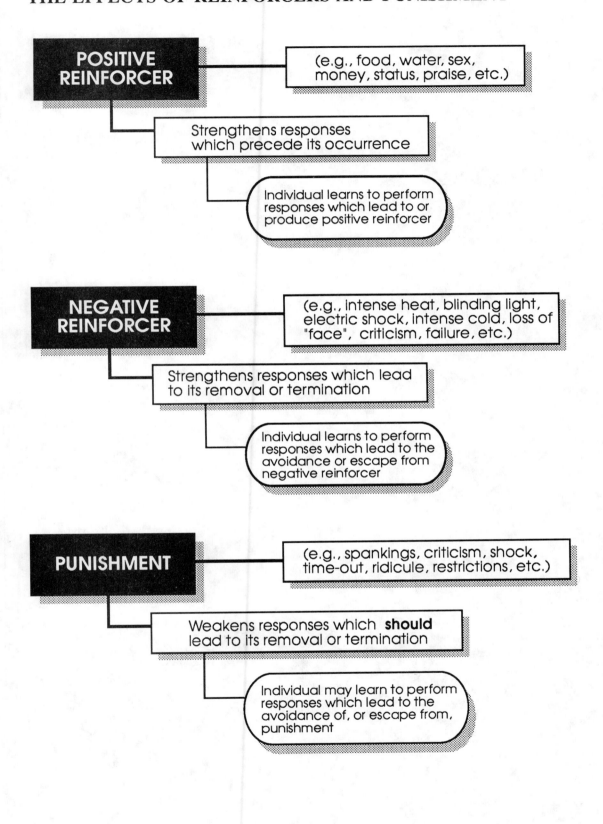

POSITIVE REINFORCER

(e.g., food, water, sex, money, status, praise, etc.)

Strengthens responses which precede its occurrence

Individual learns to perform responses which lead to or produce positive reinforcer

NEGATIVE REINFORCER

(e.g., intense heat, blinding light, electric shock, intense cold, loss of "face", criticism, failure, etc.)

Strengthens responses which lead to its removal or termination

Individual learns to perform responses which lead to the avoidance or escape from negative reinforcer

PUNISHMENT

(e.g., spankings, criticism, shock, time-out, ridicule, restrictions, etc.)

Weakens responses which **should** lead to its removal or termination

Individual may learn to perform responses which lead to the avoidance of, or escape from, punishment

BEHAVIOR PATTERNS RESULTING FROM DIFFERENT REINFORCEMENT SCHEDULES

The steeper the lines, the higher the rate of responding.

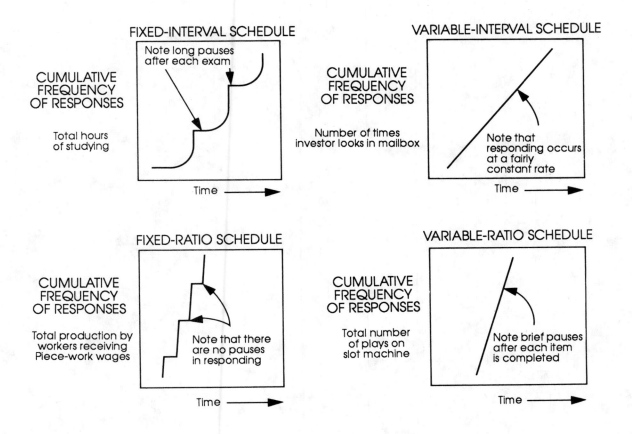

FIXED-INTERVAL SCHEDULE

CUMULATIVE FREQUENCY OF RESPONSES

Total hours of studying

Note long pauses after each exam

Time

VARIABLE-INTERVAL SCHEDULE

CUMULATIVE FREQUENCY OF RESPONSES

Number of times investor looks in mailbox

Note that responding occurs at a fairly constant rate

Time

FIXED-RATIO SCHEDULE

CUMULATIVE FREQUENCY OF RESPONSES

Total production by workers receiving Piece-work wages

Note that there are no pauses in responding

Time

VARIABLE-RATIO SCHEDULE

CUMULATIVE FREQUENCY OF RESPONSES

Total number of plays on slot machine

Note brief pauses after each item is completed

Time

THE SLOW RISE OF A RAPID-LEARNING SYSTEM

Diane Francis

Looking not at all like Russian spies who reportedly use the method to absorb complex secret codes and learn languages in as little as 24 days, students at a University of Toronto French class sink into plush swivel chairs and in a light hypnotic trance breathe in time to recorded music while a voice chants information, oscillating dramatically from a whisper to shout. Unapologetically called super-learning, the system has been around Canada and the United States for more than a decade, but during that time it has been kicked around more than its pioneers would like. The reasons are usually the very ones that seem to make it work in a society weaned on the brainwashing techniques of advertising and bent on having its soup, sex and success all in the time it takes to toast a frozen waffle. However, like pop-up waffles, it is now showing signs of being here to stay.

This spring, after a year of brisk sales in hardcover, a paperback version of *Superlearing* will join the scores of how-to titles in the bookstores. Two of its three co-authors, Canadian Sheila Ostrander and American Lynn Schroeder (the other is Ostrander's sister, Nancy), first introduced the system to the West in 1970 in a book called *Psychic Discoveries Behind the Iron Curtain*. Called suggestology in the Soviet Union and Western Europe, superlearning was developed 20 years ago by Bulgarian psychiatrist Dr. Georgi Lozanov. According to his theory, a relaxed student can soak up knowledge while in a trance and a teacher can plant posthypnotic suggestion to enable him to retrieve material instantly on command.

Several dozen universities around the world are now experimenting with super-learning and reporting positive results. In Prof. Louis Mignault's French class at the University of Toronto, students are taught yoga-like breathing techniques which are practiced in time to largo, or slow, movements by Bach, Vivaldi and other baroque composers. Then information to be learned is read three times; first by the teacher, then by a taped voice which chants in eight-second cycles (four seconds' delivery and four seconds' pause), alternating from soft to loud, and finally accompanied by the music. John Wilson, a New York school principal, took Mignault's course and mastered as much French in six weeks as most students learn in three years. In Montreal, Canadian Pacific plans to convert all employee French language programs to the method after finding that its superlearning students grasp French two to four times faster.

However, after spending about $1 million setting up superlearning courses, Ottawa's Public Service Commission maintains it is no more effective than any other process. To David Stern, director of the Ontario Institute for studies in Education's Modern Language Centre, superlearning is an unproven gimmick. But, he adds, it has some merit because relaxation eliminates emotional blocks which can impair language learning.

The government's program has failed, says Jane Bancroft, one of the method's pioneers and associate professor of French at the University of Toronto, because Bulgarian authorities refused to disclose the full details of how suggestology worked.

When authors Ostrander and Schroeder wrote their *Psychic Discoveries Behind the Iron Curtain,* details about the method were sketchy because neither had been permitted to attend classes. In 1972, the first of several Canadian government delegations went to Lozanov's Institute for Suggestology in Sofia, Bulgaria, eager to use his methods in their bilingualism programs for civil servants. Bulgarian demonstrators maintained that comfy chairs and baroque music were all that were required. However, the government wasn't the only one misled. According to the authors, one unnamed Canadian university rushed out and spent $10,000 on bean bag chairs, expecting instant miracles.

Bancroft maintains she discovered the complete method by accident, but that Ottawa ignored her advice. Authors Ostrander and Schroeder persuaded her to investigate Lozanov's institute in 1971. All three distrusted the Bulgarians' insistence that the method was so simple. After accidentally overhearing a conversation between two East German observers, Bancroft decided to sneak into their class the next day. Once inside, she realized there was a second version — one denied Westerners. These students were read material in eight-second cycles, were breathing deeply for relaxation, and the baroque pieces were from largo, or slow, sections paced at 60 beats per minute — about the rate of a normal heartbeat. Yet despite her advice and, ultimately, her protests, Ottawa offered its watered-down version in 1974, and this year will spend about two per cent of its $24 million language-training budget on superlearning-based courses.

Advertisers are already using similar techniques. Repetition, rhythm, and recital are also the three Rs of commercial production, say Morgan Earl, whose company, Morgan Earl Sounds in Toronto, creates tracks for hundreds of Canadian commercials every year. And composer-musician Lawrence Shragge of Toronto, who now writes jingles for radio and television, says he usually played music as a learning aid while he studied at university.

"Effective ads always plant a subtle posthypnotic suggestion to get viewers to buy products," says Don Schuster, a professor of psychology at Iowa State University who became convinced superlearning works after conducting a number of experiments in which students using the method were shown to improve significantly. In one case a group of beginning Spanish students learned the language two to four times faster than students using conventional methods. While the program was dropped "because it required more financial support and preparation time for teachers," Schuster admits that the similarities in advertising also frighten away educators. Say Jane Bancroft: "Sure it's a form of brainwashing. But we allow it to influence a generation of kids into buying a lot of junk foods and crummy toys and yet won't use it to provide them with an education."

Source: Originally reprinted in the February 25, 1980, edition of *Macleans's* Magazine. Reprinted here with permission.

Discussion Questions

1. Is suggestology a form of brainwashing? And if it is, given that the authors are correct that it is commonly used in advertising, should it be taught in the public school system?

2. Should there be a law concerning the use of subliminal messages in commercial advertising? products? classroom instruction?

Chapter 6
Memory

AN OVERVIEW OF MEMORY PROCESSES

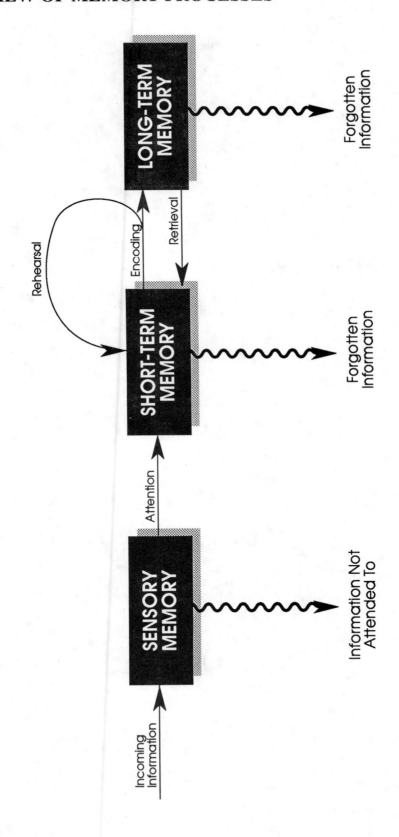

A SIMPLE RECOLLECTION TEST

Which drawing of the penny is accurate?

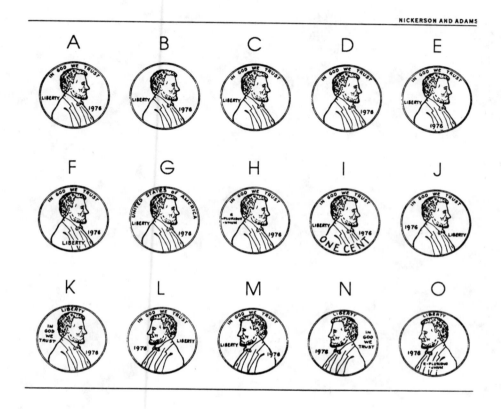

NICKERSON AND ADAMS

The correct answer is A.

Source: R. S. Nickerson and M. J. Adams. "Long-term memory for a common object," *Cognitive Psychology*, 1979: 287–307. Reprinted by permission of the authors and Academic Press.

PAIRED ASSOCIATES

Pairs of nonsense syllables, called paired associates, are used by many psychologists to study memory and forgetting. After viewing the following pairs, wait a few minutes and then look at only one column of the list. Can you remember the other member of each pair?

1. KEB — DOH

2. MEY — PAV

3. RUW — NAS

4. TIH — FEP

5. ZUN — GEQ

6. BAX — JIN

VARIETY, THE SPICE OF MEMORY

Cheryl Simon

If you're like most people old enough to remember, not only do you know where you were when John F. Kennedy was shot, but you also recall details unrelated to the event — the weather, perhaps, or what you said or wore that day.

"Why do we all remember? Something happened to us then, but what?" asks psychologist Curt Sandman. The common explanation — that the event stimulated neurochemical activity that resulted in stronger memory — prompted Sandman to experiment with a novel memory-enhancing technique. The traditional medical approach to a faltering memory encourages patients to establish and maintain routines. Instead, Sandman helps his patients with memory disorders seek variety.

Based on his findings, Sandman says, "Telling someone to establish routine to counter failing memory may be the worst advice you can give."

In the initial test of his technique, Sandman had 13 patients with severe memory disorders associated with Alzheimer's disease plan, execute and discuss a significant event with their spouse on a weekly basis. The couples engaged in events ranging from going to buy new tires to a picnic centered on selecting and sharing exotic fruits. Two to five days later, 10 of the 13 patients showed striking improvement. They recalled the day of the event four or five times better than they could a typical day and "absolutely as well as their spouses," Sandman reports.

Although the technique was designed to help the patients, their spouses, elated by the first positive shared experience in months or years, received a much-needed boost, Sandman reports. Subsequent trials reconfirmed the results: Often the patients showed perfect or near-perfect recall of the day of the significant event, whereas in the afternoon of a day in which no significant event was planned, they could not even remember what they ate for breakfast.

The goal is not to improve memory of the event per se, but of the details surrounding it. In later stages of the project, researchers will try to extend the memory-enhanced period, and to help the patients make the connections required for improved functioning.

What does this mean for the rest of us as we age? "Much age-related memory loss can be warded off if people seek activities that are different and, ideally, fun," Sandman suggests. "In other words, retirement shouldn't mean sitting around all day doing crosswords."

Discussion Questions

1. What are some of the techniques suggested by the authors for improving the memory of the elderly?

2. How well do you think these same techniques will work with younger children? with people who suffer from amnesia? with people who suffer from organic brain damage?

WEAKENED MEMORIES, BUT STRONG MINDS

When Grandpa's conversation rambles, don't jump to the conclusion that senility is setting in. His talking tangents more likely reflect a specific problem with "working memory capacity." Older people generally can understand what they read and hear as well as younger people can, and they can recall day-to-day details to function reasonably well in everyday life. These are the conclusions of a six-year study of memory and cognition in older adults conducted by Elizabeth Zelinsky, assistant professor of gerontology and psychology at the University of Southern California's Andrus Gerontology Center.

"Psychologists have known for years that remembering is a common problem among older people because of a limited working memory capacity. In conversation, it's hard for many older adults to hold what they said in memory and think of what to say next. They have trouble doing both things at once. They start to talk on one subject, change the topic, then can't go back to the original subject because they don't remember it. That's why some older people tend to ramble."

The study, funded by the National Institute on Aging, compared test results of some 600 people aged 20 to 36 with those of some 600 people aged 55 to 87. The subjects read various kinds of material to gauge their ability to understand information, for which they were timed. "Generally, the harder something is to understand, the longer it takes to read."

In one series of tests, both groups were asked to read some simple sentences such as "A flower won first prize in its category. The flower was the biggest of its kind." Reading speed was the same in both groups. When the word "daffodil" replaced the word "flower" in the second sentence, reading speed slowed for both groups — as expected, since the reader had to search through his mental dictionary to associate the specific (daffodil) with the general (flower). "The older group was no slower than the younger group. Once again, the older people understood what they read just fine." Even when more and more sentences — all related in meaning — were inserted between the first and second sentences, the older people kept pace with the younger group.

The older group tripped up when asked to read a short story. The readers had to contend with multiple topics, and the older group read far more slowly than the younger group. Zelinski concludes that older people don't have a major comprehension problem if material is in front of them. However, if they have to hold the information in memory, they tend to forget.

Other tests showed that a limited working memory capacity does not seem to affect older people in their everyday lives. "They can remember doctor's appointments, recipes, and how to get around places they visited previously."

Memory loss hits everyone in time, she adds, but there are ways to compensate: "Famed psychologist B. F. Skinner writes notes to himself and limits the amount of major thought he takes on at one time. Finally, he doesn't get upset with himself when he forgets."

Discussion Questions

1. What is a "working memory" capacity?

2. Discuss your thoughts about whether or not "working memory" loss is exclusively a function of aging. In what other situations might you find "working memory" loss?

3. What are some ways in which an elderly person might compensate for memory loss?

Chapter 7
Language, Thought, and Intelligence

AN OVERVIEW OF LANGUAGE

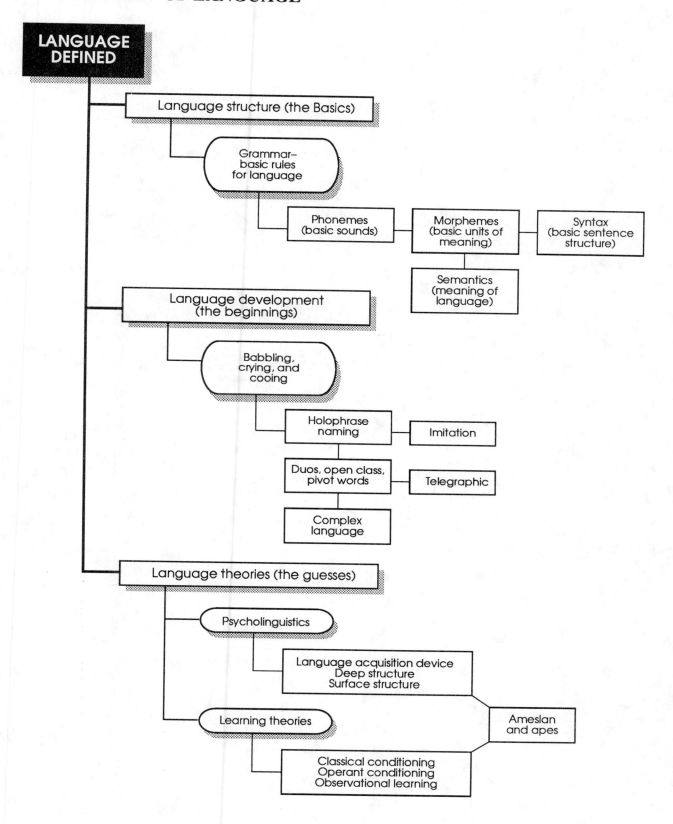

LANGUAGE DEFINED

Language structure (the Basics)

Grammar–basic rules for language

Phonemes (basic sounds)

Morphemes (basic units of meaning)

Syntax (basic sentence structure)

Semantics (meaning of language)

Language development (the beginnings)

Babbling, crying, and cooing

Holophrase naming

Imitation

Duos, open class, pivot words

Telegraphic

Complex language

Language theories (the guesses)

Psycholinguistics

Language acquisition device
Deep structure
Surface structure

Learning theories

Ameslan and apes

Classical conditioning
Operant conditioning
Observational learning

LANGUAGE STRUCTURE: Definitions and Examples

Grammar   is the systematic study of language, including morphology, syntax, phonology, semantics, and etymology.

Example: A pronoun does not always agree with its antecedent in case, but it should agree in gender, number, and person.

Phonemes   are the smallest sound units on which the language is based. Approximately 40 phonemes make up the English language.

Examples: "m" as in mat and man; "b" as in bat and boy.

Morphemes   are linguistic units of relatively stable meaning that cannot be divided into smaller meaningful parts.

Examples: most, time, no

antidisestablishmentarianism
anti-dis-establish-ment-ary-an-ism = 7 morphemes

Syntax   is the study of sentence arrangement

Example: The young boy took a red apple.

Determiner	Adjective	Noun	Verb	Determiner	Adjective	Noun
The	**young**	**boy**	**took**	**a**	**red**	**apple**

Semantics   is the study of the meanings of words.

Example: "Where have I been?" This may be a simple question, a response to a question, or an emphatic statement.

Etymology   is the study of the history of words.

Example: The word "mother" comes from the Anglo-Saxon word "modor." It is closely related to the German word "mutter" and the Sanskrit word "mata" to list a few.

TWO PROBLEMS TO SOLVE

1. How are these two rows different?

O C U P B S D G

K H I F E M N W

2. What is the next symbol in this series?

1 2 3 5 8 9 17 15 16

Answers

1. The top row contains letters with curved lines, and the bottom row contains only letters with straight lines.

2. The next number in this series is 31. Every three consecutive numbers form a series in which the first and second add together to equal the third.

AN OVERVIEW OF INTELLIGENCE

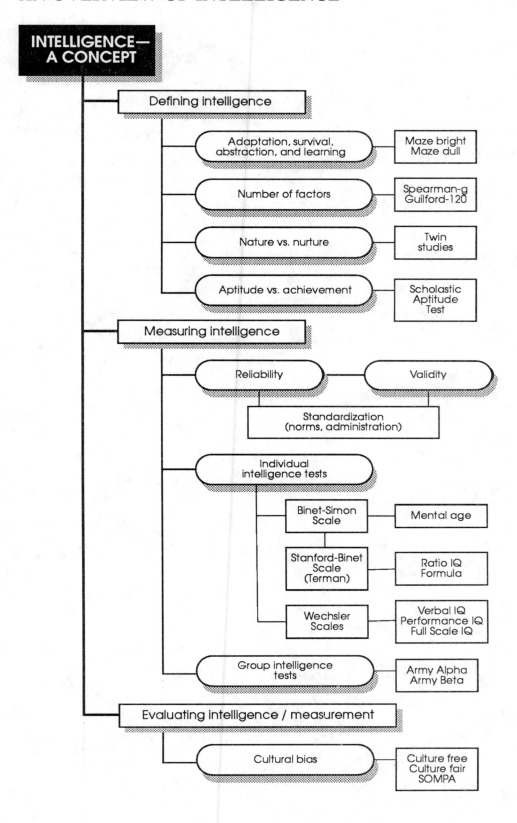

INTELLIGENCE—
A CONCEPT

Defining intelligence

- Adaptation, survival, abstraction, and learning — Maze bright / Maze dull
- Number of factors — Spearman-g / Guilford-120
- Nature vs. nurture — Twin studies
- Aptitude vs. achievement — Scholastic Aptitude Test

Measuring intelligence

- Reliability — Validity
  - Standardization (norms, administration)
- Individual intelligence tests
  - Binet-Simon Scale — Mental age
  - Stanford-Binet Scale (Terman) — Ratio IQ Formula
  - Wechsler Scales — Verbal IQ / Performance IQ / Full Scale IQ
- Group intelligence tests — Army Alpha / Army Beta

Evaluating intelligence / measurement

- Cultural bias — Culture free / Culture fair / SOMPA

IS THINKING UNCONSCIOUS ?

John Baer

Try this test: Imagine yourself standing in front of your closet, deciding what to wear to the theater. Now choose something to put on, and imagine how you'd look wearing it. Which would be better, that outfit or the one you are now wearing?

Could you do it? How did you do it? What directed your thinking process as you imagined yourself in a different place wearing different clothes, and as you then compared your appearance in that imagined scene with the one you have now? Were you aware of controlling your thoughts — of how you went about creating a mental picture, and of the procedures you used in making a judgment?

Countless philosophers and psychologists from the time of the Greeks have studied mental imagery, and it's one of the most hotly contested subjects in cognitive science today. And yet, despite this effort on the part of some of the West's finest minds, the experts in the field not only disagree on how we construct mental images; they even argue if "mind's eye" images exist at all (Gardner, 1985).

A recent argument for nonconscious thought is that of split-brain experimenter Michael Gazzaniga (1985), who theorizes that our brains are organized into relatively independent functional modules that operate without our being aware of them. What we normally consider conscious thought, he argues, typically occurs after a decision has been reached, and often without access to the line of thinking that actually occurred. Split-brain patients (in whose brains all connections between left and right hemispheres have been severed) provide dramatic examples of this. With several (but not all) of these patients, instructions directed to the right hemisphere will be carried out competently — even many tasks that involve higher-order thinking skills of analysis, synthesis, and evaluation — but the conscious subject will not know why he is doing what he is doing.

In one experiment the subject is directed, via a printed message flashed only to the right hemisphere of her brain, to leave the room. When asked why she is leaving, the subject will invariably give a plausible reason (going to the restroom, to get a drink, or to stretch her legs). The experimenter knows, of course, that this is an after-the-fact invention; but the subject, whose verbal, left-hemisphere consciousness is unaware of the instruction that has been flashed to her right hemisphere, believes that she is consciously directing her own behavior and that she has given a true account of what she is doing. Gazzaniga compares this to what we sometimes do when we rationalize our decisions and actions. Other experiments with split-brain patients demonstrate that comparing, judging, and matching-related items can all occur without subjects knowing how they did it, or even what they had done — that is without any conscious thought whatsoever (Springer and Deutsch, 1985; Gazzaniga, 1985).

Discussion Questions

1. Discuss why the results of Gazzaniga's experiments with split-brain patients are comparable to how people rationalize decisions and actions.

2. Describe what the term "split-brain" means and discuss what effects such a condition could have on a person's life.

3. Define the term "non-conscious thought" and discuss why Gazzaniga supports the theory of non-conscious thought.

WAKING SLEEPING SOULS: The Quiet Revolution in Down Syndrome

Jerry Adler
Lisa Drew

What is the real significance of Mary Boss? She is 13 years old, a sixth grader at Greenwood Lake Middle School in New York, and to all outward appearances, a human being. You would have to look under a microscope to see that she has an extra chromosome in each of her cells, resulting in the cluster of symptoms, including mental retardation, known as Down syndrome. Her speech is slurred in spots but understandable; her ambitions — to be a mountain climber and a hairdresser — not that remarkable; yet she walks among us as a living example of the inadequacies of our intellectual categories. Ask a biologist to define a human being and he might begin with the statement that a human being is an animal with 46 chromosomes in his cells. And here is Mary Boss, who has 47. People like her are, literally, expanding our definition of who is human.

It is hard to convey just how revolutionary is the sight of Mary Boss playing soccer, let alone Scrabble. Just a generation ago it was considered axiomatic that children with Down syndrome were severely retarded. The state-of-the-art medical advice was to place the infant in a state home at birth, for the good of his/her siblings and his/her parents' marriage. Raised amid unspeakable neglect in institutions like New York's Willowbrook, they lived to an average age of about 20, and died, often without so much as learning to speak. Today "it is just about out of the question" to institutionalize a Down syndrome infant at birth, according to David Rothman, professor of social medicine at Columbia University. And researchers increasingly believe most Down syndrome children fall into the mild-to-moderate range of retardation, with a few able to approach if not actually enter that realm about which parents whisper with awe and trepidation and longing: "normal."

Unimagined Potential

There was no great medical breakthrough at work; the revolution was led by parents who rebelled at surrendering their children to places that were near neighbors to dungeons. Its scientific pioneers, observes Lynn Nadel of the science advisory board of the National Down Syndrome Society, were frequently researchers who were studying something else entirely, such as language acquisition. Certain theories could be tested easily on Down syndrome patients, and, almost as a byproduct, researchers began to appreciate their ability to learn. Only in the last decade, says Nadel, with the maturing of the first generation raised at home by their parents, has it become clear that Down syndrome children "have as yet unimagined unrealized potential."

Because the field is so new, no one can say how far that potential might extend. This much has long been known about Down syndrome: that it is an inherited disorder characterized by a redundant third copy of the 21st chromosome; that it occurs approximately once in 800 to 1,000 births, about 5,000 cases a year in the United States; that it is characterized by a distinctive appearance and varying medical conditions that may include heart and immune system defects, and that the brain is always small and some degree of mental impairment is always present.

But in at least two areas there have been significant new findings from which parents can take hope.

The first of these is the critical importance of early infant stimulation. There is nothing mysterious about this technique; it means talking to, playing with, and exercising the infant — activities that are recommended for normal babies as well — but rigorously, for several hours a day. "You had to keep winding that mobile," remembers Mary Boss's father, Bill. The mobile is not to teach the baby how to tell a duck from a rabbit; it is a way of literally accessing the physical brain, of forging at an early age the neural connections that are essential for higher thought. There is even a theory that stimulation minimizes "selective neuronal debt" — the natural process in which unused cells in the brain die off in the early years of life. Normal newborns have a surplus of neurons and can afford to lose some. With smaller brains to begin with, Down syndrome infants need to exercise theirs as early as possible. "I think most Down syndrome children will be only mildly retarded or learning disabled if we can do early intervention," says Dr. Krystyna Wisniewski of New York's Institute for Basic Research in Developmental Disabilities.

The other discovery is that, whether or not you can make Down syndrome (children) smarter, you can certainly make them appear that way by improving their language skills. Virtually all Down syndrome children have serious problems with receptive and expressive language. This is partly the result of hearing loss, owing to their propensity for ear infections, and partly the result of poor coordination and articulation. But Laura Meyers, a linguist at UCLA, believes there is a deeper problem, an inability to perform the rapid auditory processing needed to understand spoken English. "They get left out of the dialogue," she says; "their brains are not getting the information needed to understand language." In particular, she believes that Down syndrome children simply don't hear short, unstressed words, which includes most of the articles and prepositions that hold the language together.

The solution, she believes, lies in the computer, augmented with a voice synthesizer. In one of her studies, toddlers are presented with special keyboards with pictures of toys and actions; they learn to swat the appropriate picture to communicate simple wants and ideas. In another study, school-age Down syndrome children have regular keyboards and a more ambitious agenda: to learn syntax and grammar. They say things like "Want go Donald Tom'." On the screen, the words that slip by so quickly in conversation are captured and made visible; the measured and uninflected voice of the synthesizer renders them audible. It is a gross heresy in education to proceed from written language to spoken, rather than the other way round. But try telling that to Ralph Bingener, a 17-year old with Down syndrome. "Why do you like writing on computers?" Meyers asks him; and he replies, "My ideas are really fruitful on the computer."

Getting Dressed

The growing acceptance of programs such as Meyers's have given rise to a new phenomenon, the Down syndrome computer jock. Matthew Costa, six, first started working on a keyboard at three, knew his alphabet at four, and scores average on a test of reading recognition. He has been in a "trainable" class, where he learns simple life skills such as getting dressed and crossing the street, but Wisniewski is urging Matthew's parents to put him in a more demanding "educable" program. The choice of a program can be a difficult one for parents, torn between wanting their children to learn as much as possible and the need for them to practice buttoning, zipping and toothbrushing. Mary Boss was in regular classes through fourth grade, and then, reluctantly, moved to a learning-disabled program; her reading and English have kept up, but she has fallen behind in math.

And for the future? Mary knows she is different, of course, but she doesn't see it as an impediment to happiness. "I'll be a mother, of course," she says. "When I get older, I'll marry my boyfriend, which is Gary...when we both get older, make that. We stick together, me and Gary, because we both have Down syndrome and stuff." Whether or not she will marry, it is considered unlikely that she — or any Down syndrome patient — will ever be completely independent. "I'm not sure that's the goal," says Nadel. "The ability to live in their own apartment and balance their checkbook is not the issue." Matthew's mother has what is considered a realistic goal for a Down syndrome child, to live in a supervised group home, help with the cooking and go to a vocational program during the day. Modest, except by comparison to what his fate would have been just a generation ago: to sit on a chair in a musty day room and mutely stare at the wall until he died. "That they used to institutionalize these guys just amazes me," his mothers says. "Thank God it didn't happen to him."

Discussion Questions

1. Discuss why the parents of a newborn child with Down syndrome might be wise to imitate Mary Boss's father's conduct of "winding that mobile"?

2. Discuss how it is possible to "make Down syndrome children appear smarter".

Chapter 8
Motivation and Emotion

AN OVERVIEW OF MOTIVATION

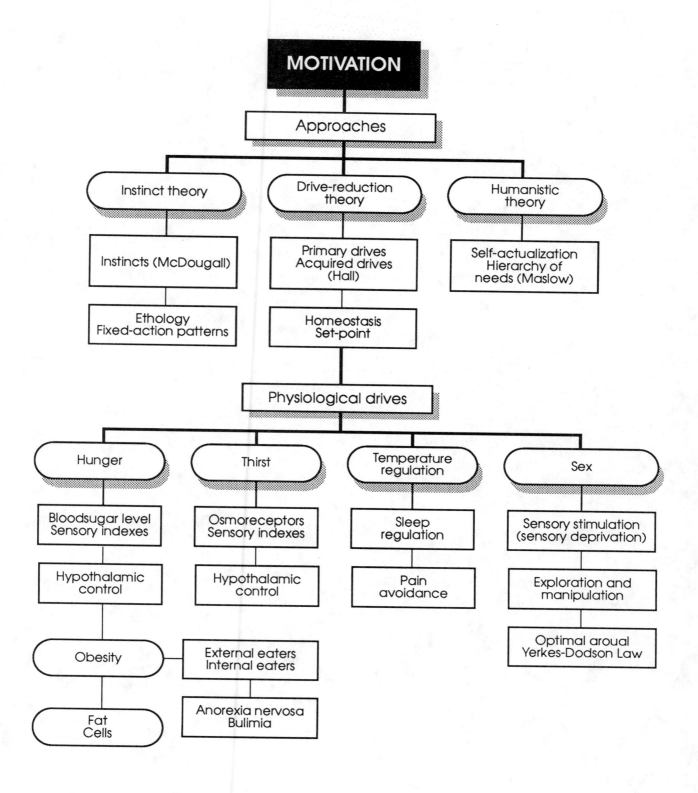

MOSLOW'S HIERARCHY OF NEEDS

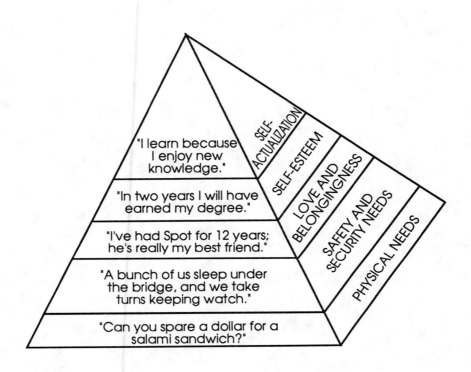

COUNTING CALORIES

Calories Expended in One Hour of Activity as a Function of Body Weight

	Body Weight				
Activity	100 lbs.	125 lbs.	150 lbs.	175 lbs.	200 lbs.
Sleeping	40	50	60	70	80
Sitting quietly	60	75	90	105	120
Standing quietly	70	88	105	123	140
Eating	80	100	120	140	160
Driving, light housework	95	119	143	166	190
Desk work	100	125	150	175	200
Walking slowly	133	167	200	233	267
Walking rapidly	200	250	300	350	400
Swimming	320	400	480	560	640
Running	400	500	600	700	800

What about you? How many calories do you burn up during the day? You can use the approximations given in the above chart to make an estimate. Let's follow Paul, a rather sedentary office worker, through a typical weekday. He takes down his pocket calculator *after* dinner and jots down his weight: 150 pounds. First he notes that he sleeps about eight hours a night. As we see in the chart, 8 X 60 (the approximate number of calories a 150-pound person burns up by sleeping for an hour) = 480. Then he notes that he spends about six hours a day at desk work. He eats for about an hour, plus or minus a few minutes, but this is only an estimate. Oh yes, he drives for perhaps an hour a day. That adds up to 16 hours.

"Well," he admits to himself, "if the truth be known, I sit quietly for about five hours a day watching television or reading." He works on hobbies (desk work) for another two hours, and exercises by walking rapidly for another hour or so per day. Thus, he burns up approximately 2,768 calories in a typical 24-hour day.

AN OVERVIEW OF SOCIAL MOTIVATIONS

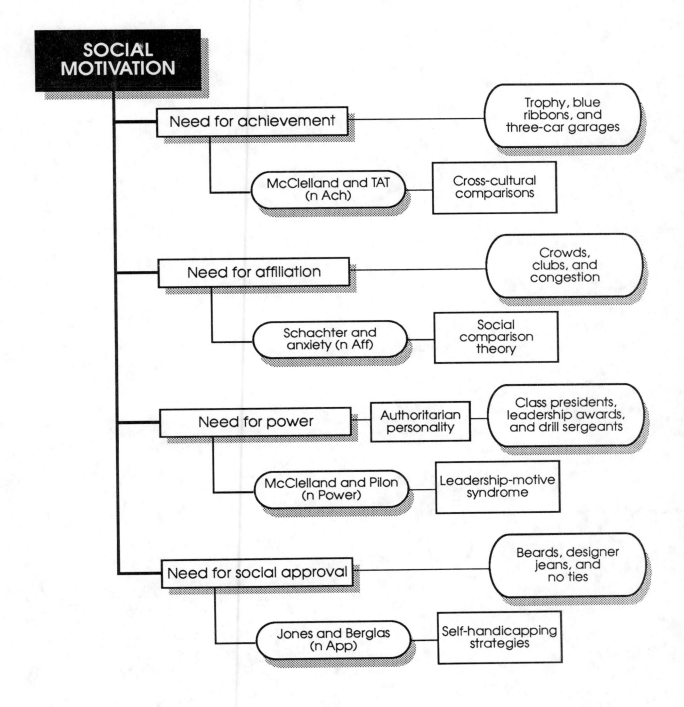

SOCIAL MOTIVATION

Need for achievement — Trophy, blue ribbons, and three-car garages

McClelland and TAT (n Ach) — Cross-cultural comparisons

Need for affiliation — Crowds, clubs, and congestion

Schachter and anxiety (n Aff) — Social comparison theory

Need for power — Authoritarian personality — Class presidents, leadership awards, and drill sergeants

McClelland and Pilon (n Power) — Leadership-motive syndrome

Need for social approval — Beards, designer jeans, and no ties

Jones and Berglas (n App) — Self-handicapping strategies

AN OVERVIEW OF EMOTIONS

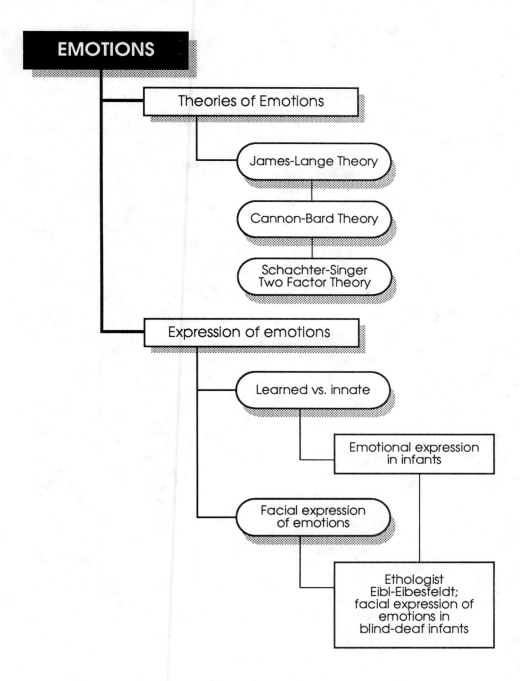

WHY KIDS GET FAT: A New Study Shows Obesity Is in the Genes

Where do fat children come from? For the most part, they are the product of overweight parents. But if that connection is obvious, the reasons behind it have remained elusive. Have the kids inherited their girth? Or do children get fat simply because they follow the eating habits of their parents? Over the years, as part of the nature vs. nurture argument, scientists have deadlocked on those questions. But last week a U.S. and Danish team tilted the scales again, announcing that after studying 540 adopted children in Denmark they concluded that obesity is mostly built into the genes and not the psyche.

The evidence, as reported in the *New England Journal of Medicine,* was unequivocal: the size of the children consistently reflected the size of the natural parents. There was absolutely no correlation between the body builds of the adoptees and their surrogate mothers and fathers. And these parallels held true in all weight classes, from skinny to grossly fat.

The study was conducted by a team led by Dr. Albert J. Stunkard, a psychiatrist and obesity specialist at the University of Pennsylvania School of Medicine. Using Denmark's uncommonly complete, computerized record of its five million residents, researchers found 540 adults who had been adopted at an early age. The subjects were questioned about their general health, including height and weight. Using a "body-mass index" (weight divided by the square of the height), the investigators divided the participants into four groups: thin, median, overweight and obese. Biological and adoptive parents of each subject were then similarly surveyed and the data fed into a computer at the University of Texas Health Science Center in Houston. When he couldn't find a relationship between the size of the adoptive parents and their children, Stunkard had his controversial result: "Childhood family environment alone has little or no effect" on obesity.

Some investigators remain unconvinced. "This study shows that body proportions resemble those of the biological parents," says University of Michigan anthropologist Stanley Garn. "It still doesn't answer the question of the genetic inheritance of fatness." To support his doubts, Garn points to his own study, published in the early 1970's, in which he examined 160 adopted children up to the age of 20. He found that they resembled their adoptive parents in degree of obesity about as much as did children raised by their own parents.

Optimistic conclusion: But if obesity is inherited, what hope does a fat person have to reduce? A good deal, according to Stunkard: he suggests that the children of overweight parents could be targeted for intensive weight-control measures, particularly vigorous exercise programs, thereby neutralizing their inherited propensity. "Such persons," he notes, "can already be identified with some assurance: 80 percent of the offspring of two obese parents become obese." Such notions are the backbone of the University of Pennsylvania's new weight-loss program for black teenage girls. At 12, Jessica Cunningham is 5 feet 4 and weighs 235 pounds. Her mother weighs "200-plus pounds" and her sister had a similar weight problem when she was Jessica's age. The psychologists who run the project think they can get Jessica down to 160 pounds after four months of effort. And if they're right, Cunningham will prove Stunkard's one truly optimistic conclusion: "Genes," he says, "are not destiny."

Discussion Questions

1. Identify and discuss the reasons (listed in the article) that people become obese. Do you agree or disagree? Are there any other reasons you can think of?

2. Given that Dr. Stunkard's hypothesis about obesity genes is correct, what other genetic disorders/syndromes can be modified or manipulated environmentally?

Source: Matt Clark with Connie Leslie in Philadelphia, *Newsweek*, February 3, 1986. All rights reserved. Reprinted by permission.

Chapter 9
Development

AN OVERVIEW OF DEVELOPMENT

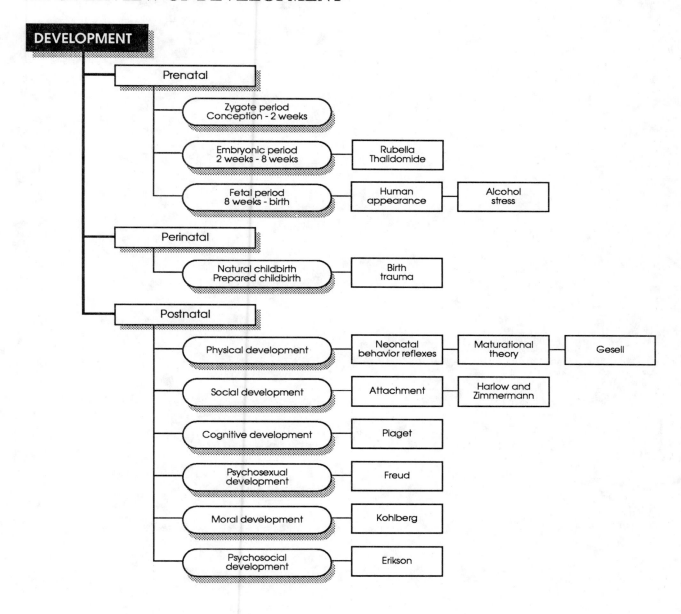

MILESTONES OF INFANT MOTOR DEVELOPMENT

Behavior	Average age at which it is performed
Child can raise chin from ground	1 month
Child can sit with support	4 months
Child can sit alone	7 months
Child can stand by holding onto furniture	9 months
Child can crawl	10 months
Child can walk when held by hand and led	11 months
Child can stand alone	14 months
Child can walk alone	15 months

Note that these are average figures. Most children will vary from them in some respect.

PIAGET'S STAGES OF COGNITIVE DEVELOPMENT

Approximate Age (years)	Stage	Characteristics
0–2	Sensorimotor	Motor meaning Object permanence Beginning of symbolic representation (language)
2–7	Preoperational	Language develops Naive realist No conservation Cannot "reason" or explain why (nonlogical thinking) Egocentric
7–13 (puberty)	Concrete Operational	Can conserve Concept formation Understands rules Differentiates between self and world Moralistic No abstract thinking
13+	Formal Operational	Abstract thinking Manipulates abstract concepts Hypothetical reasoning Higher order reasoning Creative language use

KOHLBERG'S STAGES OF MORAL DEVELOPMENT

Level	Stage
Level One	*Pre-Conventional*
Step 1	Punishment and obedience orientation. Obey rules to avoid punishment.
Step 2	Instrumental–relativist orientation. Conform to obtain rewards, have favors returned.
Level Two	*Conventional*
Step 3	Good boy/nice girl orientation. Conform to avoid disapproval or dislike by others.
Step 4	Law and order orientation. Conform to avoid censure by authorities.
Level Three	*Post Conventional*
Step 5	Social contract – legalistic orientation. Morality of contract, individual rights and democratically accepted law. Conform to maintain community welfare.
Step 6	Universal ethical principle orientation. Morality of individual principles of conscience. Conform to avoid self-condemnation.

THREE MORAL DILEMMAS

1. Recently in Massachusetts, parents of a child with leukemia, Chad Green, were forced into taking their child for painful chemotherapy by the courts. They had wished to treat him with the experimental drug Laetrile and high doses of vitamins. Later it turned out that they *were* also treating Chad with Laetrile and vitamins, even though the court ordered them to stop because of possible poisoning from these chemicals. Rather than discontinue a treatment they considered essential, Chad's parents took him to Tijuana, Mexico, where he continued to receive Laetrile and vitamins, along with chemotherapy. Chad's parents acted in direct opposition to the court order that prevented them from leaving Massachusetts or directing their son's medical treatment. Legally, they could have been prosecuted for kidnapping. Do you believe they acted morally? Why?

2. A woman in a Nazi concentration camp during World War II was able to save her family from execution and starvation by having sexual intercourse with the German officers who ran the camp. Do you believe she acted morally? Why?

3. A moral problem: "In Europe a woman was near death.... There was one drug that the doctors thought might save her.... [It] was expensive to make, but the druggist was charging ten times what the drug cost him to make.... The sick woman's husband...went to everyone he knew to borrow the money, but he could only get together...about half of what it cost.... So [the husband] got desperate and broke into the [drugstore] to steal the drug for his wife." (From Kohlberg.) Do you believe he acted morally? Why?

Source: *Adjustment and Growth: The Challenges of Life,* p. 194, by Spencer Rathus and Jeffrey Nevid. Copyright 1980 by Holt, Rinehart and Winston, Inc.

ERIKSON'S STAGES OF PSYCHOSOCIAL DEVELOPMENT

Psychological State	Task or Crisis	Social Conditions	Psychological Outcome
Stage 1: Oral–sensory (birth to 1 year)	Can I trust the world?	Support and provision of basic needs	Basic Trust vs Distrust
		Lack of support and deprivation	
Stage 2: Muscular–anal (2–3 years)	Can I control my own behavior?	Permissiveness and support	Autonomy vs Shame and doubt
		Overprotection and lack of support	
Stage 3: Locomotor–genital (4–5 years)	Can I become independent of my parents by exploring my limits?	Encouragement to explore	Initiative vs Guilt
		Lack of opportunity to explore	
Stage 4: Latency (6–11 years)	Can I master the necessary skills to adapt?	Adequate training and encouragement	Industry vs Inferiority
		Poor training and lack of support	
Stage 5: Puberty and adolescence (12–18 years)	Who am I? What are my beliefs, feelings, and attitudes?	Internal stability and positive feedback	Personal identity vs Role confusion
		Confusion of purpose and unclear feedback	
Stage 6: Young Adulthood (young adulthood)	Can I give fully of myself to another?	Warmth and sharing	Intimacy vs Isolation
		Lonliness	
Stage 7: Adulthood (adulthood)	What can I offer succeeding generations?	Purposefulness and productivity	Generativity vs Stagnation
		Lack of growth and regression	
Stage 8: Maturity (maturity)	Have I found contentment and satisfaction through my life's work and play?	Unity and fulfillment	Integrity vs Dispair
		Disgust and dissatisfaction	

ATTITUDES TOWARD AGING TEST

Circle **T** (True) or **F** (False) for each of the following questions.

T F 1. By age 60 most couples have lost their capacity for satisfying sexual relations.

T F 2. With advancing age people become more externally oriented, less concerned with self.

T F 3. As individuals age they become less able to adapt satisfactorily to a changing environment.

T F 4. General satisfaction with life tends to decrease with age.

T F 5. As people age they tend to become more homogeneous, i.e., all old people tend to be alike.

T F 6. For the older person, having a stable intimate relationship is no longer highly important.

T F 7. The aged are more susceptible to a wider variety of psychological dysfunctions than young and middle-aged adults.

T F 8. Most older people are depressed much of the time.

T F 9. Church attendance increases with age.

T F 10. The occupational performance of the older worker is typically less effective than that of the younger adult.

T F 11. Most older people are just not able to learn new skills.

T F 12. When forced to make a decision, elderly persons are more cautious and take less risk than younger persons.

T F 13. Compared to younger persons, aged people tend to think more about the past than the present or future.

T F 14. Most elderly people are unable to live independently and reside in nursing-home-like institutions.

For answers, consult Handout 9.8, "Facts on Aging," the 14 items of which correspond to the 14 questions above.

FACTS ON AGING

These facts correspond to each question on the Attitudes Toward Aging Test.

1. For most healthy couples the capacity for satisfying sexual relations continues into the 70s and 80s. Important for both sexes is active and frequent sexual expression of some type (Kimmel, p. 216).

2. With advancing age, there is a shift toward increased internalization. As the salience of external factors decreases, the importance of inner processes increases. There is more concern with one's own emotions and physical functions — an inner-world orientation (Kimmel, pp. 305–306).

3. General adaptive characteristics differ between individuals regardless of age. Little predictable change in adaptional characteristics occurs. Through middle and old age personality traits remain generally consistent and the adaptive interaction between person and social environment remains stable (Kimmel, p. 308).

4. In general there is no noticeable decline in life satisfaction with age. Disease, social losses, and personality characteristics are more important than age in creating dissatisfaction with life (Kimmel, pp. 316, 320).

5. Older people show similar developmental changes just as children, adolescents, etc., do. However, they remain individuals and are no more alike than all young or middle-aged people are alike (Kimmel, p. 317).

6. An intimate relationship — having a confidant to buffer against losses — is highly important for older persons. Depression is less likely and life satisfaction is greater for older people with such a relationship (Kimmel, p. 317).

7. Young, middle, and old are all subject to the same range of psychopathology. There is not much difference in incidences of neuroses or psychoses (Kimmel, p. 326).

8. Mild depression occurs in old age as it does at all ages. One study reported only one fifth of healthy older respondents were rated by psychiatrists as mildly depressed (Kimmel, p. 326).

9. Although no decline in religious beliefs occurs with age, a decline in church attendance does. Possibly religion becomes more internally practiced or a decline in health makes church attendance more difficult (Kimmel, p. 357).

10. Slowed reaction time and impaired ability to master new problems not relevant to past experience are unlikely to affect the average person's occupational performance up to age 60. Because older people are likely to choose situations where experience is valuable rather than development of new approaches, their performance is generally as effective as that of younger adults (Kimmel, p. 378).

11. For continued learning, health, education, and individual differences are more important than age. Up to 65 there is little decline in learning or memory ability and thus little reason an elderly person cannot learn as well as younger individuals. It may simply take a little longer to learn the same material (Kimmel, p. 381).

12. Although more likely to choose a "no risk" problem solution if available, if *not* available, older subjects take the same amount of risk as younger subjects. If forced to decide, older people are as likely to choose "high risk" solutions as are younger people (Kimmel, p. 383).

13. Older persons do not think more about the past than younger people. Past thoughts are not more prevalent than present or future ones for the aged (Kimmel, p. 414).

14. Most older persons are community residents. At any one time only four to five percent reside in nursing homes (Kimmel, p. 459).

Source: D. C. Kimmel, *Adulthood and Aging: An Interdisciplinary, Developmental View* (New York: Wiley, 1974). Copyright © 1974 John Wiley and Sons, Inc. Reprinted by permission.

FIVE PHASES OF DYING

1. **DENIAL,** or refusal to accept the fact that one is dying.

2. **ANGER,** the phase when one protests the fact of death and wonders, "Why me?" A sense of unfairness and injustice is often manifested by open hostility toward doctors, nurses, and loved ones.

3. **BARGAINING,** the phase during which one recognizes the inevitability of death and bargains for time.

4. **DEPRESSION,** the phase characterized by expressions of self-pity, sorrow, and grief.

5. **ACCEPTANCE,** which one experiences under optimal conditions. The preceding phases have been worked through successfully, and death is met with peace and tranquility.

PREVENTING EARLY BIRTHS
Prenatal Care Not Only Works, It's A Bargain

Terence Monmaney

Marvel at the neonatal intensive-care nursery, the artificial womb where hopes and babies incubate and usually survive. But how many of the infants there could be spared the affliction that lands them in so precarious a state? While birth disorders such as genetic diseases and developmental defects are practically unavoidable (short of early diagnosis in the womb and abortion), a large fraction of premature and underweight births appear preventable.

About 75,000 to 100,000 newborns enter intensive care each year primarily because they are underdeveloped or merely too small to thrive, weighing less than five-and-a-half pounds, according to an analysis by the congressional Office of Technology Assessment. Researchers led by Paul A. Buescher of the North Carolina Center for Health Statistics recently confirmed that prenatal care can prevent the birth of many underweight babies; their study, published in the *American Journal of Public Health,* found that women who received less adequate care were 30 percent more likely to have a preemie than those with access to a full-service prenatal program. "This is basically not a medical problem," comments Rae K. Grad, executive director of the National Commission to Prevent Infant Mortality, which was created by Congress last year. "It's a social problem with medical consequences."

Low birth weight is a rare social problem in that it seems cheaper to address than ignore. Dozens of studies show that providing free care to poor pregnant women more than pays itself back; it cuts down on high-tech rescues of preterm babies and on the expense of treating the approximately one in six newborns who leave the ICN with a physical or mental disability. An analysis of some California clinics showed that for every Medicaid dollar spent on prenatal care, nearly $2 was saved from the burden of underweight babies. In Virginia, researchers estimated that if adequate pregnancy care were universally available, the state would eventually spend $49.8 million less each year treating mental retardation linked to low birth weight. As the OTA concluded, "For every low birthweight birth averted by earlier or more frequent prenatal care, the U.S. health-care system saves between $14,000 and $30,000."

Health experts do not agree on precisely what constitutes adequate prenatal care. The American College of Obstetricians and Gynecologists recommends that a pregnant woman visit her doctor 13 to 15 times in the course of a normal 37- to 40-week gestation, beginning with one visit early in the first trimester and progressing to weekly checkups. But prevention is not an exact science; many women who appear unlikely to have an underweight baby still do, even with top-notch care. The best that doctors and healthcare workers can do is counsel pregnant women to avoid the known risk behaviors and watch closely those expectant mothers predisposed to early labor.

Risks: Cigarette smoking, alcohol consumption, marijuana, malnutrition, and severe chronic stress add to a woman's chances of having a preterm or underweight baby; so does hypertension, diabetes, and being under 28 or over 35. Combining such risk factors further worsens the odds; the nation's highest rates of low birth weight and infant mortality occur among black teenage mothers.

Warnings: A backache, vaginal discharge, and palpable uterine contractions are some of the signs of imminent premature labor. If such warnings persist, a pregnant woman should consult her doctor, who may administer a drug (ritodrine, for example) which can arrest labor in some cases, provided it hasn't gone too far.

More risks: This group includes women carrying twins, women with a history of preterm birth or abortion, and those with certain abnormalities of the uterus or cervix. A controversial device, known as a tocodynamometer, has been developed for such high-risk women. It detects those contractions that can lead to labor even before a woman feels them. The monitor straps around her waist to record uterine muscle action; the stored information is sent over the phone to the maternity ward for interpretation. If labor appears imminent, drugs may then be administered in an attempt to forestall it. The OTA concludes that the experimental monitor has not yet been proven to reliably prevent early births.

Electronics can't win the battle against low birth weights, the leading cause of infant mortality. "We're in love with high-tech solutions," says Lynda Johnson Robb, LBJ's daughter, Virginia's former first lady and a member of the National Commission to Prevent Infant Mortality. "But what we really need is the political will to do something about the problem." There are signs that whatever will we had has faded. From 1978 to 1984, the number of children in families with no medical insurance rose by 30 percent, to 24 percent of all kids. Meanwhile, federal funding to key sources of maternal care dropped by a third. The fall in coverage has put maternity services out of reach of more women, as indicated by a recent rise in the number who have had no prenatal care — which boosts the likelihood of preterm birth two- to fivefold. Dr. Vanessa Haygood, medical director of the Guilford County family planning and maternity clinic in Greensboro, N.C., is puzzled by the neglect: "Why not take care of the pregnant women rather than treat the complications of their premature babies?" Indeed. Why be stingy when it's clear the investment saves money as well as lives.

Discussion Questions

1. Discuss the pros and cons of socialized health care (given the information in this article).

2. Should prenatal health care be legislated? Should there be penalties/consequences if a woman refuses or fails to seek out prenatal care?

Chapter 10
Personality

AN OVERVIEW OF PERSONALITY THEORIES

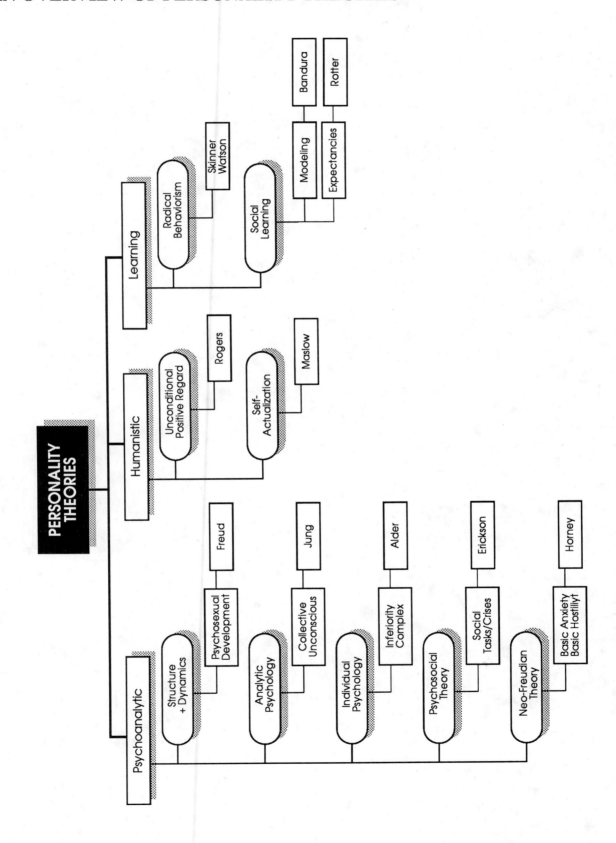

BEHAVIOR DETERMINANTS TEST

For each of the following items, Circle **A** if you agree with the statement, and **D** if you disagree.

A D 1. In understanding behavior the emphasis should be on learning rather than biological factors.

A D 2. Really good newspaper people have an instinct for "where it's happening."

A D 3. Being raised in an enriched environment can have a positive effect on intelligence.

A D 4. Understanding behavior can best be done by studying a small number of fundamental building blocks out of which behavior is constructed.

A D 5. Behavior is primarily shaped through the laws of conditioning.

A D 6. "Mothering" in humans is a learned behavior, not the result of a maternal instinct.

A D 7. Learning is more important than instinct for human survival.

A D 8. Some people are naturally more athletic than others.

A D 9. There are basic ability differences between the sexes that no amount of training can overcome.

A D 10. An animal cannot be taught to do things that are extremely dissimilar to what it would instinctively do in its natural environment.

A D 11. The sum of behavior is more than its individual parts.

A D 12. We are all born with a collective consciousness that helps guide our behavior.

A D 13. If a child is born of drug-addicted parents, it is destined to become a drug addict even if not raised by those parents.

A D 14. Behavior is typically a product of learned wants and needs.

A D 15. People like professional wine tasters and perfume smellers are born with extraordinary discrimination abilities.

A D 16. Extremely obese people are born with an unusually strong drive to eat.

A D 17. Creativity is something you can learn.

A D 18. One's biological parents are a more important determiner of intelligence than one's raising parents.

A D 19. A good memory is something one develops with practice.

A D 20. Men are naturally more mechanically minded than women.

A D 21. Innate drives such as need for food, sex, and water are more important determiners of human behavior than needs for love, prestige, and money.

A D 22. Your IQ may change as you age; it is not set at birth.

A D 23. Your brain is not a fixed entity; i.e., it can be changed, strengthened, or expanded through learning.

A D 24. The ability to understand mathematics is more instinctively a male than a female trait.

A D 25. Aggression is really a learned behavior rather than a survival instinct.

A D 26. The most important factor in suffering a heart attack is a predisposition toward heart attacks rather than environmental stresses.

A D 27. Personality traits are developed over time; i.e., you are not born to be of a certain personality type.

A D 28. Much of our behavior is controlled by an unconscious, instinctual component of personality.

A D 29. We are not predisposed to be introverted or extroverted; it is a behavior learned through modeling and reinforcement.

A D 30. Women are not naturally more emotional than men.

A D 31. Pathological reactions to today's stresses are most heavily influenced by a predisposition (that runs in families) to react that way.

A D 32. Good coordination is more a learned than an innate ability.

A D 33. The most important determinant of musical talent is one's early environment rather than the specific family one is born into.

A D 34. Basic psychological urges derive from innate biological needs such as hunger and sex.

FREUD'S MODEL OF PERSONALITY

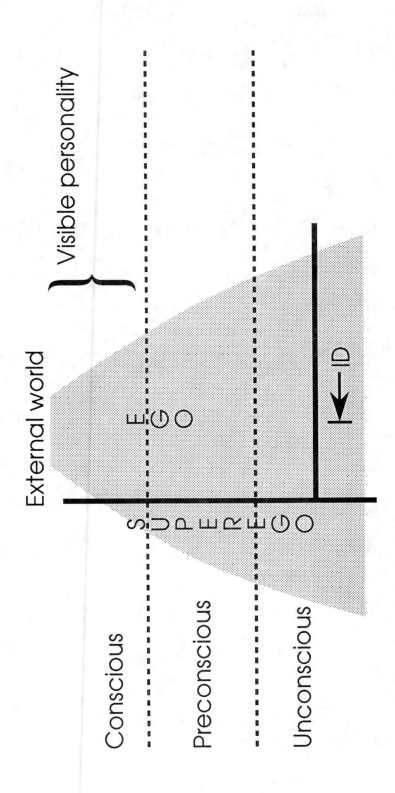

FREUD'S STAGES OF PSYCHOSEXUAL DEVELOPMENT

Stage of Psychosexual Development	Erogenous Zone	Activity	Potential Later Personality
Oral (0–1 year)	Mouth	Sucking; incorporation biting	Oral-incorporative; "sucker", aggressive; oral sadistic
Anal (2–3 years)	Anal sphincter	Urge for elimination; strict toilet training reward	Anal-retentive or expulsive; productive; creative
Phallic (4–5 years)	Genital organs	Masturbation; Oedipus complex; Electra complex	Identification, later functional relationships with men and women
Latency (6–puberty)	None	Same-sexed relationships	Functional long-term relationships with same sex, further refinement of identification
Genital (puberty–adulthood)	Genital organs	Sexual desire, sexual relationships	Socialization, genuine friendships; stable, mature, long-term relationships; vocational choice

COMMON EGO DEFENSE MECHANISMS

Denial	The unwillingness to accept or face an unpleasant event
Repression	Banishing of anxiety-arousing thoughts and feelings from consciousness
Regression	Retreat to an earlier, more comfortable stage of development
Projection	Attributing to others one's own threatening impulses, hostilities, etc.
Rationalization	Self-justifying explanations offered in place of the real, more threatening, unconscious reasons for one's behaviors
Reaction Formation	Expression of feelings that are the opposite of the anxiety-arousing unconscious feelings
Identification	Adoption of the same-sex role behaviors, mannerisms, and actions
Sublimation	Rechanneling of unacceptable impulses into socially approved activities

MEAURING SELF-ACTUALIZATION

For each item, select the alternative that is most like you.

1. a.   I prefer to save good things for future use.
    b.   I prefer to use good things now.

2. a.   My moral values are dictated by society.
    b.   My moral values are self-determined.

3. a.   I often make my decisions spontaneously.
    b.   I seldom make my decisions spontaneously.

4. a.   It is important that others accept my point of view.
    b.   It is not necessary for others to accept my point of view.

5. a.   I try to be sincere, but I sometimes fail.
    b.   I try to be sincere, and I am sincere.

6. a.   I have a problem in fusing sex and love.
    b.   I have no problem in fusing sex and love.

7. a.   People are both good and evil.
    b.   People are not both good and evil.

8. a.   I find some people who are stupid and uninteresting.
    b.   I never find any people who are stupid and uninteresting.

9. a.   I am afraid to be tender.
    b.   I am not afraid to be tender.

Source: Reproduced with permission of Education and Industrial Testing Service; copyright 1963, EDITS, San Diego, CA: Personal Orientation Inventory.

AN OVERVIEW OF ASSESSMENT

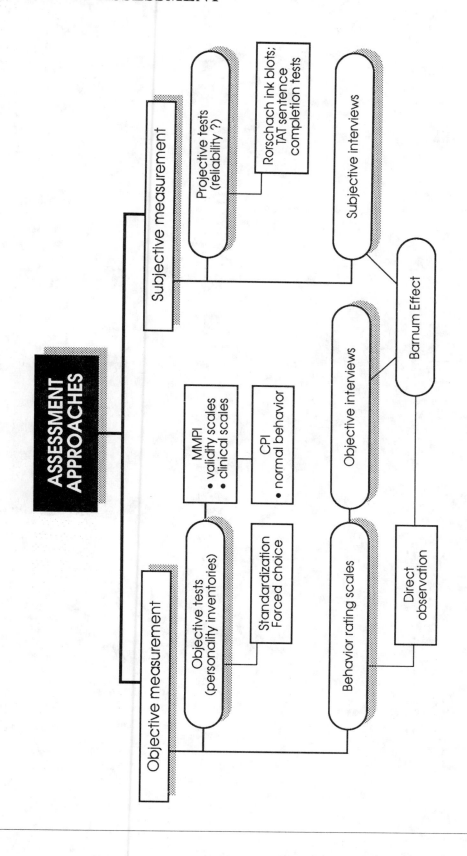

INKBLOTS SIMILAR TO THOSE USED IN THE RORSCHACH TEST

PERSONALITY — IS IT ALL IN YOUR GENES?

Carol Tavris

You might think that people could agree that everyone is a product of both heredity and environment, but the origin-of-personality debate persists. Now, two lines of research are adding controversial evidence to the heredity side of the equation.

Does personality change with age? As part of the Baltimore Longitudinal Study of Aging, Paul T. Costa, Jr., Ph.D., and Robert R. McCrae, Ph.D., both of the Gerontology Research Center of the National Institute on Aging, have been exploring the dimensions of personality that seem to be particularly stable after age thirty. They have identified five key personality traits — extroversion, neuroticism, openness to experience (including curiosity and need for variety), agreeableness, and conscientiousness — that seem impervious to aging, experience, or even emotional maturation.

Of course, because most personality tests are self-administered, it is possible they do not measure the stability of personality but the stability of one's self-concept. To examine this possibility, Costa and McCrae also asked spouses to rate each other's traits and again found strong consistency over time. These five central traits, they conclude, are "still stable after all these years."

The Genetics of Personality. The main ingredients of personality may be constant, by why — genetics or environment? In a bombshell study published recently, Auke Tellegen, Ph.D., and a research team at the University of Minnesota report that environment counts for almost nothing in the development of key personality traits, including the "big five."

These results are based on the Minnesota Twin Study, a project that has been studying identical and fraternal twins — some reared together and some apart — from 1970 to 1986. Over the years, Tellegen and his team have been giving the twins personality inventories and examining the relative contribution to personality of genetics, shared family environment, and "unshared environment," a grab-bag category that includes an individual's unique experiences, perceptions, and mood fluctuations, as well as errors in measurement. They found that about half of the diversity in personality can be attributed to genetics, and most of the rest comes from the idiosyncratic category.

"The Minnesota Twin Study reminds us that people are not made of *Play-Doh,* squished into any shape by any environment," says Carole Wade, Ph.D., of the College of Marin, who has been reviewing the research on genetics and personality. "But it is equally ludicrous to conclude that environment counts for nothing." Moreover, some traits, such as self-esteem and achievement motivation, do change over time. Even traits that do have a heritable component, such as aggression, are not necessarily fixed for life: many aggressive little boys grow into unaggressive young men, and many aggressive young men become gentler with age. So although researchers long to separate heredity from environment for scientific purity, the question may never be resolved.

Discussion Questions

1. Which five personality characteristics are said to remain stable over time?

2. Can there be a true separation between environment and heredity in the question of personality? Why?

PERSONALITY'S PART AND PARCEL

Paul Chance

Some say there are two kinds of people. What kind of people would say that?

There are," he said, "two kinds of people: idea people and feeling people. I think you're an idea person."

My speech professor was trying to cheer me up after one of the more humiliating experiences in a humiliating freshman year. He had this idea that people would become better public speakers if they first practiced doing really silly things in front of a group. He had me stand before the class, one foot in front of the other, and rock back and forth while swinging my arms, ape fashion, and chanting "Aaahhoooo, aaahhooo." I did it, but I did it with the embarrassed stiffness you might expect from Richard Nixon if you made him moon walk. Like I said, it was humiliating.

The prof's philosophical musings were intended to reassure me. "You'll never make it as an actor," he was saying, "but you might make it in some more bookish occupation." I took the personality assessment in stride and immediately began wondering (as befitted my bookish personality) whether the entire human population really could be categorized by this, or any other two-legged taxonomy. Was it really true that there were only two kinds of people in the world?

I had problems with the feeling and idea pigeonholes right from the start. I couldn't help wondering why, if I was an idea person, I was in danger of flunking out of college. Was it because my classes placed little emphasis on ideas? I did do better in subsequent years, when the ideas became more plentiful and interesting than they had been in my freshman speech class. But somehow the idea–feeling theory of personality seemed to lack predictability.

Another problem I ran into was that there were lots of competing theories about the two kinds of people in the world. One familiar idea is that everybody is either an optimist or a pessimist. Optimists are sure that they'll never die, and that if they do die they'll wake up to the glory of heaven. Pessimists are sure that they won't live much longer, and that if they wake up in heaven, they won't like it.

Some people believe that everybody can be described according to which end of a scale of mental health they fall on. Those who like this theory refer to people on one end of the scale as all together, tightly wrapped and the like, while those on the other end of the scale are coming apart, loosely wrapped and so on. Those who like this way of classifying people almost always feel they have it all together, but some of them are really loosely wrapped.

Another theory says that people are either realists or idealists. A realist is a person who knows which side of the bread is buttered; an idealist has more important things to worry about. The consensus is that realists eat better than idealists.

Other folks divide the human race into animal people and plant people, depending upon the company they keep. Animal people talk to their furry or feathered companions in melodious tones about everything from the price of cheese to American foreign policy, as if the animals understood every word that was said. Plant people find such displays sentimental and silly, and they expound upon their views in great detail to their annual and perennial friends.

Humans can also be classified as either people people (as in, "He's a people person") or thing people ("She's great with machines"). People people are often said to have a lot of personality, which implies something uncomplimentary about thing people. There's a song that hints at a similar classification of people. It says that people who need people are the luckiest people in the world. People who don't need people are not so lucky. Obviously the song was written by a people person.

Sigmund Freud had his own theory about the two kinds of people. He believed that personality consists of id, ego, and superego. The id is the instinctual "I want it," the superego is the guilt-ridden "You can't have it," and the ego is the rational "Let's see what we can work out." If I've read Freud correctly, the compromising ego prevails in almost no one. That means most of us are either id people or superego people, infantile or guilt-ridden.

Carl Jung, Freud's most famous disciple, divided humans into introverts and extroverts. You might think introverts and extroverts are rather like idea people and feeling people, respectively, but they aren't. Introverts are sometimes more interested in feelings than in ideas (poets, for instance), and extroverts are sometimes very unfeeling (used car dealers who turn back odometers). Introverts and extroverts are basically what other people call loners and joiners.

In recent years we've heard a lot about Type A and Type B personalities. Type B people eat lunch at home or in a restaurant and take their time about it. Type A people ram down a hot dog while running up an escalator. Type A people work harder at making money than Type B people, but they don't know how to enjoy it. Type B people know how to enjoy money but aren't sure it's worth the bother to get it.

Of course, the idea that everyone can be tagged with one of two labels doesn't appeal to everybody. There are lots of psychologists, for example, who would argue that there aren't 2 kinds of people, or 6, or 8, or 37. There are as many kinds of people as there are people. And each person may be different kinds of people at different times. Being a human being is a complicated business, these psychologists argue, and you cannot arbitrarily squeeze everybody into one of two categories.

Despite these doubts, I think there is some merit to the idea that there are two kinds of people. In fact, I've come up with my own theory. I propose that there are two kinds of people in the world: those who believe there are two kinds of people and those who don't.

I place myself in the second category. How about you?

Discussion Questions

1. What category would you place yourself in?

2. What is *your* theory of personality?

Chapter 11
Health Psychology

AN OVERVIEW OF STRESS

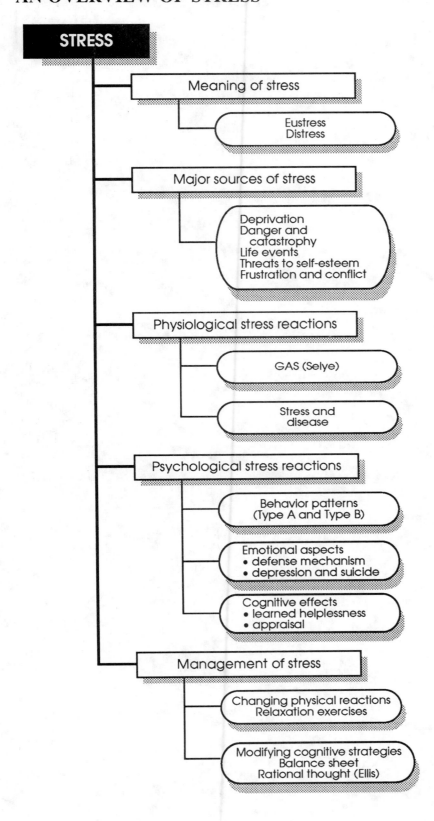

STRESS

- Meaning of stress
  - Eustress
  - Distress

- Major sources of stress
  - Deprivation
  - Danger and catastrophy
  - Life events
  - Threats to self-esteem
  - Frustration and conflict

- Physiological stress reactions
  - GAS (Selye)
  - Stress and disease

- Psychological stress reactions
  - Behavior patterns (Type A and Type B)
  - Emotional aspects
    - defense mechanism
    - depression and suicide
  - Cognitive effects
    - learned helplessness
    - appraisal

- Management of stress
  - Changing physical reactions
    Relaxation exercises
  - Modifying cognitive strategies
    Balance sheet
    Rational thought (Ellis)

THE COLLEGE SCHEDULE OF RECENT EXPERIENCES

How stressful has your last year been? How many changes have you gone through? In order to compare the amount of stress you have experienced with that of other college students, fill out the following schedule by noting the number of times you experienced each event and then multiplying this number by the indicated number of life-change units. Add up your total score and look below.

College Schedule of Recent Experiences

Indicate the number of times during the last 12 months you:	Life-Change Units	Item Score
1. entered college _____	X 50 =	_____
2. married _____	X 77 =	_____
3. had either a lot more or a lot less trouble with your boss _____	X 38 =	_____
4. held a job while attending school _____	X 43 =	_____
5. experienced the death of a spouse _____	X 87 =	_____
6. experienced a major change in sleeping habits (sleeping a lot more or a lot less, or changing the part of the day in which you sleep) _____	X 34 =	_____
7. experienced the death of a close family member _____	X 77 =	_____
8. experience a major change in eating habits (a lot more or a lot less food intake, or very different meal hours or surroundings) _____	X 30 =	_____
9. made a change in or choice of major field of study _____	X 41 =	_____
10. revised your personal habits (friends, dress, manners, associations) _____	X 45 =	_____
11. experienced the death of a close friend _____	X 65 =	_____
12. were found guilty of minor violation of the law (such as traffic tickets or jaywalking) _____	X 22 =	_____
13. had an outstanding personal achievement _____	X 40 =	_____
14. experienced pregnancy, or fathered a pregnancy _____	X 68 =	_____
15. had a major change in the health or behavior of a family member _____	X 56 =	_____
16. had sexual difficulties _____	X 58 =	_____
17. had trouble with in-laws _____	X 42 =	_____
18. had a major change in the number of family get-togethers (a lot more or a lot less) _____	X 26 =	_____

Indicate the number of times during the last 12 months you:	Life-Change Units	Item Score
19. had a major change in financial state (a lot worse off or a lot better off than usual). _____	X 33 =	_____
20. gained a new family member (through birth, adoption, older person moving in) _____	X 50 =	_____
21. changed your residence or living conditions _____	X 42 =	_____
22. had a major conflict in or change in values _____	X 50 =	_____
23. had a major change in church activities (a lot more or a lot less frequently than usual). _____	X 36 =	_____
24. had a marital reconciliation with your mate. _____	X 58 =	_____
25. were fired from work _____	X 62 =	_____
26. were divorced _____	X 76 =	_____
27. changed to a different line of work _____	X 50 =	_____
28. had a major change in the number or arguments with spouse (either a lot more or a lot less than usual) _____	X 50 =	_____
29. had a major change in responsibilities at work (promotion, demotion, lateral transfer) _____	X 47 =	_____
30. had your spouse begin or cease work outside the home _____	X 41 =	_____
31. had a major change in working hours or conditions _____	X 42 =	_____
32. had a marital separation from your mate _____	X 74 =	_____
33. had a major change in usual type and/or amount of recreation _____	X 37 =	_____
34. had a major change in the use of drugs (a lot more or a lot less) _____	X 52 =	_____
35. took a mortgage or loan less than $10,000 (as for purchase of a car, TV, or school loan) _____	X 52 =	_____
36. had a major personal injury or illness _____	X 65 =	_____
37. had a major change in the use of alcohol (a lot more or a lot less) _____	X 46 =	_____
38. had a major change in social activities _____	X 43 =	_____
39. had a major change in the amount of participation in school activities _____	X 38 =	_____
40. had a major change in the amount of independence and responsibility (for example, budgeting time) _____	X 49 =	_____

Indicate the number of times during the last 12 months you:

	Life-Change Units	Item Score
41. took a trip or a vacation _____	X 33 =	_____
42. were engaged to be married _____	X 54 =	_____
43. changed to a new school _____	X 50 =	_____
44. changed dating habits _____	X 41 =	_____
45. had trouble with school administration (instructors, advisors, class scheduling, and so on). _____	X 44 =	_____
46. broke or had broken a marital engagement or steady relationship. _____	X 60 =	_____
47. had a major change in self-concept or self-awareness. _____	X 57 =	_____
TOTAL SCORE		_____

Source: Adapted from Anderson (1972) by Marx et al. (1975), copyright © 1975 by Pergamon Press Ltd.

How did you do?

Marx, Garrity, and Bowers (1975) found that half the students in one college sample obtained scores above 767, with scores ranging form 42 to 3890. The same students were surveyed on the extent of medical illness they had experienced during the 60-day period preceding the interview. Students with high life-change scores showed a higher incidence of disorders ranging from pimples, rashes, chest pains, and headaches to bruises and blisters than students with low scores.

Taking a STABS at It:
THE (ABBREVIATED) SUINN TEST ANXIETY BEHAVIOR SCALE

How does your level of test anxiety compare to those of others? Take the twenty STABS items below, and then score your answers according to the key provided by your instructor.

Items from the Suinn Test Anxiety Behaviors Scale

The items in the questionnaire refer to experiences that may cause fear or apprehension. For each item, place a check (✔) under the column that describes how much you are frightened by it nowadays. Work quickly but be sure to consider each item individually.

Item	Not at all	A little	A fair amount	Much	Very much
1. Rereading the answer I gave on the test before turning it in.	_____	_____	_____	_____	_____
2. Sitting down to study before a regularly scheduled class.	_____	_____	_____	_____	_____
3. Turning in my completed test paper.	_____	_____	_____	_____	_____
4. Hearing the announcement of a coming test.	_____	_____	_____	_____	_____
5. Having a test returned.	_____	_____	_____	_____	_____
6. Reading the first question on a final exam.	_____	_____	_____	_____	_____
7. Being in class waiting for my corrected test to be returned.	_____	_____	_____	_____	_____
8. Seeing a test question and not being sure of the answer.	_____	_____	_____	_____	_____
9. Studying for a test the night before.	_____	_____	_____	_____	_____
10. Waiting to enter the room where a test is to be given.	_____	_____	_____	_____	_____
11. Waiting for a test to be handed out.	_____	_____	_____	_____	_____
12. Waiting for the day my corrected test will be returned.	_____	_____	_____	_____	_____
13. Discussing with the instructor an answer I believed to be right but which was marked wrong.	_____	_____	_____	_____	_____
14. Seeing my standing on the exam relative to other people's standing.	_____	_____	_____	_____	_____

Item	Not at all	A little	A fair amount	Much	Very much
15. Waiting to see my letter grade on the test.	_____	_____	_____	_____	_____
16. Studying for a quiz.	_____	_____	_____	_____	_____
17. Studying for a midterm.	_____	_____	_____	_____	_____
18. Studying for a final.	_____	_____	_____	_____	_____
19. Discussing my approaching test with friends a few weeks before the test is due.	_____	_____	_____	_____	_____
20. After the test, listening to the answers my friends selected.	_____	_____	_____	_____	_____

Normative Data for the Suinn Test Anxiety Behavior Scale

To attain your total STABS score, assign points to check marks in the five columns as follows:

Not at all	1
A little	2
A fair amount	3
Much	4
Very much	5

You may want to include items on which you scored 4 or 5 in a rational restructuring program (pp. 226–227). Then add all the numbers to arrive at a total score.

Richard Suinn (1969) attained a mean score of 122.00 for a longer, 50-item version of this questionnaire. This was from a sample of 158 students who were enrolled in a Colorado state university.

We administered the 20-item questionnaire to a sample of 248 male and female undergraduate students at Northeastern University in 1979. The majority of the sample was white, but there were 28 blacks, 3 Orientals, and 14 Hispanic Americans. Our norms were as follows:

Raw STABS Score	Percentile
68	95
61	80
57	75
52	60
49	50
45	35
41	25
38	20
32	10

CONFLICT TYPE IDENTIFICATION: A MATCHING EXERCISE

———— 1. Paula has developed into a top notch skier and genuinely looks forward to her weekend ski trips. She works with a local industry as a clerk typist. She is aware of a job opening in the industry that would involve a promotion and a handsome salary increase, but the position calls for weekend duties.

———— 2. Belinda is currently dating a young man to whom she is very attracted; however, he is much shorter than she is, which causes her some embarrassment. She is introduced to Jerome, a tall handsome young man, who is a struggling artist.

———— 3. Bob is awakened in the middle of the night with a horrendous toothache. On the way to the dentist the next morning, he fearfully recalls his last visit and the "less than pleasant" experiences he had.

———— 4. A person caught between a rock and a hard place.

———— 5. Darryl arrives to pick up his date for the first time. He is met at the door by his date's oldest brother and his pet python. The brother gives him a bear hug and threatens him with harm if he makes any advances toward his sister. Darryl really enjoys the date and finds Naomi very attractive.

Match the people above with the conflict types listed below.

Conflict Types

A. Approach–Approach

B. Avoidance–Avoidance

C. Approach–Avoidance

Answers

1. Approach–Approach (a)
2. Approach–Avoidance (c)
3. Avoidance–Avoidance (b)
4. Avoidance–Avoidance (b)
5. Approach–Avoidance (b)

FULL-LENGTH PROGRESSIVE RELAXATION INSTRUCTIONS

Before you relax, create a conducive setting. Settle down on a reclining chair, a couch, or a bed with a pillow. Pick a time and place where you are unlikely to be interrupted. Be sure that the room is warm and comfortable. Dim the lights. Loosen any tight clothing.

Use the instructions below (Wolpe & Lazarus, 1966) to relax. Each time you tense a muscle group, tighten it about two-thirds as hard as you could if you were using maximum strength. The feeling that a muscle may go into a spasm is a signal that you are tensing it too hard. When you let go of your tensions, do so completely.

The instructions can be memorized, tape-recorded, or read aloud by a friend or relative. An advantage to having them read rather than taping them is that the reader can always slow down or speed up according to some prearranged signal—such as lifting one finger to indicate slowing down and two fingers to indicate speeding up.

Relaxation Instructions

Relaxation of Arms (time: 4–5 minutes)

Settle back as comfortably as you can. Let yourself relax to the best of your ability …Now, as you relax like that, clench your right fist, just clench your fist tighter and tighter, and study the tension as you do so. Keep it clenched and feel the tension in your right fist, hand, forearm…and now relax. Let the fingers of your right hand become loose, and observe the contrast in your feelings…Now, let yourself go and try to become more relaxed all over …Once more, clench your right fist really tight. ..hold it, and notice the tension again…Now let go, relax; your fingers straighten out, and you notice the difference once more…Now repeat that with your left fist. Clench your left fist while the rest of your body relaxes; clench that fist tighter and feel the tension…and now relax. Again enjoy the contrast…Repeat that once more, clench the left fist, tight and tense…Now do the opposite of tension — relax and feel the difference. Continue relaxing like that for a while…Clench both fists tighter and tighter, both fists tense, forearms tense, study the sensations…and relax: straighten out your fingers and feel that relaxation. Continue relaxing your hands and forearms more and more…Now bend your elbows and tense your biceps, tense them harder and study the tension feelings…all right, straighten out your arms, let them relax and feel that difference again. Let the relaxation develop…Once more, tense your biceps; hold the tension and observe it carefully…Straighten the arms and relax; relax to the best of your ability…Each time, pay close attention to your feelings when you tense up and when you relax. Now straighten your arms, straighten them so that you feel most tension in the triceps muscles along the back of your arms; stretch your arms and feel the tension…And now relax…Get your arms back into a comfortable position. Let the relaxation proceed on its own. The arms should feel comfortably heavy as you allow them to relax…Straighten the arms once more so that you feel the tension in the triceps muscles: straighten them. Feel that tension…and relax. Now let's concentrate on pure relaxation in the arms without any tension…Get your arms comfortable and let them relax further and further. Continue relaxing your arms ever further. Even when your arms seem fully relaxed, try to go that extra bit further; try to achieve deeper and deeper levels of relaxation.

Relaxation of Facial Area with Neck, Shoulders, and Upper Back (time: 4–5 minutes)

Let all your muscles go loose and heavy. Just settle back quietly and comfortably. Wrinkle up your forehead now; wrinkle it tighter…And now stop wrinkling your forehead, relax and smooth it out. Picture the entire forehead and scalp becoming smoother as the relaxation increases…Now frown and crease your brows and study the tension…Let go of the tension again. Smooth out the forehead once more…Now, close your eyes tighter and tighter…feel the tension…and relax your eyes. Keep your eyes closed, gently, comfortably, and notice the relaxation…Now clench your jaws, bite your teeth together; study the tension throughout the jaws…relax your jaws now. Let your lips part slightly…Appreciate the relaxation…Now press your tongue hard against the roof of your mouth. Look for the tension…All right, let your tongue return to a comfortable and relaxed position…Now purse your lips, press your lips together tighter and tighter…Relax the lips. Note the contrast between tension and relaxation. Feel the relaxation all over your face, all over your forehead and scalp, eyes, jaws, lips, tongue and throat. The relaxation progresses further and further…Now attend to your neck muscles. Press your head back as far as it can go and feel the tension in the neck; roll it to the right and feel the tension shift; now roll it to the left. Straighten your head and bring it forward, press your chin against your chest. Let your head return to a comfortable position, and study the relaxation. Let the relaxation develop…Shrug your shoulders, right up. Hold the tension…Drop your shoulders and feel the relaxation. Neck and shoulders relaxed…Shrug your shoulders again and move them around. Bring your shoulders up and forward and back. Feel the tension in your shoulders and in your upper back…Drop your shoulders once more and relax. Let the relaxation spread deep into the shoulders, right into your back muscles; relax your neck and throat, and your jaws and other facial areas as the pure relaxation takes over and grows deeper, deeper…ever deeper.

Relaxation of Chest, Stomach, and Lower Back (time: 4–5 minutes)

Relax your entire body to the best of your ability. Feel that comfortable heaviness that accompanies relaxation. Breathe easily and freely in and out. Notice how the relaxation increases as you exhale…as you breathe out just feel that relaxation… Now breathe right in and fill your lungs; inhale deeply and hold your breath. Study the tension…Now exhale, let the walls of your chest grow loose and push the air out automatically. Continue relaxing and breathe freely and gently. Feel the relaxation and enjoy it…With the rest of your body as relaxed as possible, fill your lungs again. Breathe in deeply and hold it again…That's fine, breathe out and appreciate the relief. Just breathe normally. Continue relaxing your chest and let the relaxation spread to your back, shoulders, neck and arms. Merely, let go…and enjoy the relaxation. Now let's pay attention to your abdominal muscles, your stomach area. Tighten your stomach muscles, make your abdomen hard. Notice the tension…And relax. Let the muscles loosen and notice the contrast…Once more, press and tighten your stomach muscles. Hold the tension and study it…And relax. Notice the general well-being that comes with relaxing your stomach…Now draw your stomach in, pull the muscles right in and feel the tension this way…Now relax again. Let your stomach out. Continue breathing normally and easily and feel the gentle massaging action all over your chest and stomach…Now pull your stomach in again and hold the tension… Now push out and tense like that; hold the tension…once more pull in and feel the tension…now relax your stomach fully. Let the tension dissolve as the relaxation grows deeper. Each time you breathe out, notice the rhythmic relaxation both in your lungs and in your stomach. Notice thereby how your chest and your stomach relax more and more…Try and let go of all contractions anywhere in your body…Now direct your attention to your lower back. Arch up your back, make your lower back quite hollow, and feel the tension along your spine…and settle down comfortably again relaxing the lower back…Just arch your back up and feel the tensions as you do so. Try to keep the rest of your body as relaxed as possible. Try to localize the tension throughout your lower back area…Relax once more, relaxing further and further. Relax your lower back, relax your upper back, spread the relaxation to your stomach, chest, shoulders, arms and facial area. These parts relaxing further and further and further and ever deeper.

Relaxation of Hips, Thighs, and Calves Followed by Complete Body Relaxation

Let go of all tensions and relax…Now flex your buttocks and thighs. Flex your thighs by pressing down your heels as hard as you can…Relax and note the difference…Straighten your knees and flex your thigh muscles again. Hold the tension…Relax your hips and thighs. Allow the relaxation to proceed on its own. . . Press your feet and toes downwards, away from your face, so that your calf muscles become tense. Study that tension…Relax your feet and calves…This time, bend your feet towards your face so that you feel tension along your shins. Bring your toes right up…Relax again. Keep relaxing for a while…Now let yourself relax further all over. Relax your feet, ankles, calves and shins, knees, thighs, buttocks, and hips. Feel the heaviness of your lower body as you relax still further…Now spread the relaxation to your stomach, waist, lower back. Let go more and more. Feel that relaxation all over. Let it proceed to your upper back, chest, shoulders and arms and right to the tips of your fingers. Keep relaxing more and more deeply. Make sure that no tension has crept into your throat; relax your neck and your jaws and all your facial muscles. Keep relaxing your whole body like that for a while. Let yourself relax.

Now you can become twice as relaxed as you are merely by taking in a really deep breath and slowly exhaling. With your eyes closed so that you become less aware of objects and movements around you and thus prevent any surface tensions from developing, breathe in deeply and feel yourself becoming heavier. Take in a long, deep breath and let it out very slowly…Feel how heavy and relaxed you have become.

In a state of perfect relaxation you should feel unwilling to move a single muscle in your body. Think about the effort that would be required to raise your right arm.

As you think about raising your right arm, see if you can notice any tensions that might have crept into your shoulder and your arm… Now you decide not to lift the arm but to continue relaxing. Observe the relief and the disappearance of the tension…

Just carry on relaxing like that. When you wish to get up, count backwards from four to one. You should then feel fine and refreshed, wide awake and calm.

Letting Go Only

Once you have practiced progressive relaxation through alternate tensing and letting go, you will probably find that you can relax completely through letting go only. Simply focus on the muscle groups in your arms and allow them to relax. Just keep letting go. Allow the sensations of relaxation, warmth, and heaviness to develop on their own. Repeat for your facial area with your neck, shoulders, and upper back; for your chest, stomach, and lower back; and for your hips, thighs, and calves.

You will find that you can skip over many of the instructions. Relaxation in one area can be allowed to "flow" into relaxation in another. Give yourself instructions that feel right to you.

You can probably achieve deep relaxation through letting go in only about five minutes. Then simply continue to relax and enjoy the sensations fully for another ten to twenty minutes. Now and then you can go on a "mind trip" through your body to seek out pockets of residual tension and let them go. We recommend that you return to the full-length Wolpe and Lazarus instructions once every couple of months to renew your awareness of the sensations of bodily tensions. This will keep relaxation skills "sharp."

Once you have learned how to relax, you can call on your skills as needed, letting go of bodily tensions when you want that alarm turned down. You can also relax once or twice daily to reduce high blood pressure and cut down on Type A behavior.

One may also be instructed in methods of muscle relaxation and breathing control in preparation for childbirth. They are essential ingredients of the Lamaze method of natural childbirth.

Source: Relaxation instructions reprinted from Wolpe and Lazarus (1966), pp. 177–180. Published by Pergamon Press Ltd.

HOW PSYCHOLOGICAL FACTORS CAN CAUSE PHYSICAL ILLNESS

How does personality affect illness? That's what specialists in health psychology are trying to learn. It now appears that our personalities affect every aspect of disease, from its prevention to how well we comply with treatment.

- After suffering a heart attack, one personality type — known as "angry-moody" — took considerably longer than others to seek help from a doctor, according to a study by University of Miami psychologist Sally Kolitz. Sixty-five percent of them waited at least 14 hours to consult a physician, despite great pain.

- Among men, the personality characteristic known as "John Henryism" — working hard to master one's environment — seems connected to high blood pressure, based on research by Neil Schneiderman, director of behavioral medicine at the University of Miami and editor of Health Psychology.

- Suspicious, aggressive people may survive for a long time in nursing homes while cheerful, cooperative people may die very quickly. Morton Lieberman and Sheldon Tobin, University of Chicago psychologists, have discovered.

- Jack Tapp, an adjunct professor of health psychology at the University of Miami, finds that mind imagery (imagining yourself into a happier, calmer state), progressive muscle relaxation, biofeedback, transcendental meditation, or prayer all can help a person gain a sense of control over his or her body and life, and improve general health.

Health psychology is part of broader efforts to plumb the relationships between body, mind, and personality. "The more we look, the more complex it is," noted University of Miami psychologist Catherine Green. Not long age, when medical researchers announced their discovery that angry, impatient, hostile people— now called "Type A" personalities — were most prone to heart attack, health psychology rose to higher visibility.

"Virtually all illness can be modified by the perceptions, feeling, experiences of the individual patient," Green believes. Asthma can be triggered by mood. Cold sore can be brought on by emotional pressure. One study found that cervical cancer is correlated to perception of life stress. Depression often promotes poor health. "Some views of the world almost inoculate you against illness. The hardy personality, certain ways of seeing the world, seeing problems and ourselves, definitely give an advantage."

Discussion Questions

1. Reflecting back, can you identify illnesses you may have had which might have resulted from your emotional state?

2. Brainstorm on possible mind–body relationships for the following diseases:

   1. migraine headaches

   2. body rash

   3. eye problems

   4. congestion

   5. constipation

Food for Thought

While there are no absolute answers to #2, some suggestions might be:

1. **migraine headaches** — poor self image, feelings of unworthiness

2. **body rash** — fear of interpersonal relationships, wanting to shield self from others/situations

3. **eye problems** — an unwillingness to see things clearly

4. **congestion** — an unwillingness to say something that needs to be said

5. **constipation** — holding on to old "gunk", an unwillingness to let go of the past.

Chapter 12
Abnormal Psychology

AN OVERVIEW OF ABNORMALITY

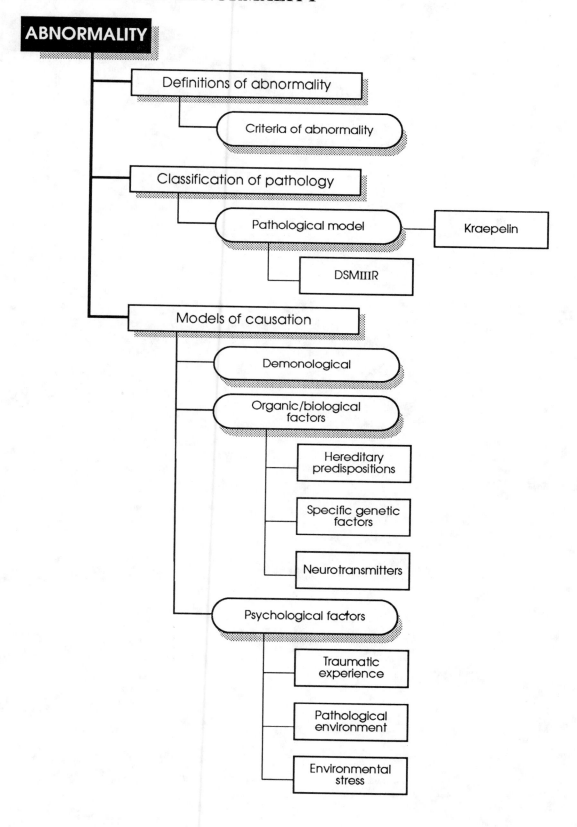

DSM III–R CLASSIFICATIONS (CONDENSED)

AXIS I (Any mental disorders that may be present)

1. *Organic Mental Disorders*
   - dementia
   - substance induced
2. *Psychoactive Substance Use Disorders*
   - dependence
   - abuse
3. *Schizophrenic Disorders*
   - catatonic
   - disorganized
   - paranoid
   - undifferentiated
   - residual
4. *Paranoid Disorders*
   - delusional paranoia
   - ertomanic
   - grandiose
   - jealous
   - persecutory
   - somatic
5. *Mood Disorders*
   - bipolar
   - mixed manic depressive
   - major dysthymia
6. *Anxiety Disorders*
   - panic
   - social phobia
   - simple phobia
   - obsessive-compulsive
   - post traumatic stress
   - generalized anxiety

7. *Somatoform Disorder*
   - body dysmorphic
   - conversion (hysterical neorosis)
   - hypochondriasis
   - somatization
   - psychogenic pain
8. *Dissociative Disorder (or hysterical neurosis, dissociative type)*
   - multiple personality
   - psychogenic fugue
   - psychogenic amnesia
   - depersonalization
9. *Psychosexual Disorder*
   - paraphilias
   - sexual dysfunctions
10. *Sleep Disorder*
    - dyssomnia
    - parasomnia
11. *Impulse Control Disorder*
    - Intermittent explosive
    - Kleptomania
    - pathological gambling
    - pyromania
    - trichotillomania
12. *Adjustment Disorders*
    - with anxious mood
    - with depressed mood
    - with disturbance of conduct

AXIS II (Any personality disorder that may be present)

- paranoid
- schizoid
- schizotypal
- antisocial
- borderline
- histrionic
- narcissistic
- avoidant
- dependent
- obsessive-compulsive
- passive aggressive

AXIS III (Any medical or physical disorder that may also be present)

AXIS IV (A 7-point scale rating the severity of psychological and social factors that may have place the individual under stress, ranging from 1 (none) to 7 (catastrophe)

AXIS V (A 7-point scale rating the individual's recent success in coping with his or her stress, ranging from 1 (superior) to 7 (grossly impaired)

ZUNG'S SELF-RATING DEPRESSION SCALE

Whether we describe it as feeling blue, or hopeless, or withdrawn, we have each experienced what psychologists label depression. In fact, depression has been called by psychologists the "common cold of psychopathology." Of all the emotional problems available to us, depression is one of the most common. We have all experienced the depression from the loss of a loved one, from a separation from our friends, or from our failures. Such depression is normal and, being normal, it is usually transitory and specific to a certain situation. The important thing for us to know about our depressive feelings is the level and pervasiveness of those feelings. A scale which gives us that knowledge can be very beneficial.

A similar need led psychiatrist William Zung to develop his Self-Rating Depression Scale. During a research project measuring the relationship of depression and arousal during sleep, Dr. Zung found the available measures of depression inadequate. He wrote, "These inadequacies related to factors such as length of a scale being too long and too time-consuming, especially for a patient who is already depressed and having psychomotor difficulties." His model for a scale required that it be easily completed by the person involved, and that it serve as an accurate measure of how the person was feeling at that particular time.

Below are 20 statements about feelings each of us has at one time or another. Read each one and place a check in the column which best describes how you are feeling at this time.

Statement	None or a little of the time	Some of the time	A good part of the time	Most or all of the time
1. I feel downhearted, blue, and sad.				
2. Morning is when I feel best.				
3. I have crying spells or feel like it.				
4. I have trouble sleeping through the night.				
5. I eat as much as I used to.				
6. I enjoy looking at, talking to, and being with attractive women/men				
7. I notice that I am losing weight.				
8. I have trouble with constipation.				
9. My heart beats faster than usual.				
10. I get tired for no reason.				
11. My mind is clear as it used to be.				
12. I find it easy to do the things I used to do.				
13. I am restless and can't keep still.				
14. I feel hopeful about the future.				

Statement	None or a little of the time	Some of the time	A good part of the time	Most or all of the time
15. I am more irritable than usual.				
16. I find it easy to make decisions.				
17. I feel that I am useful and needed.				
18. My life is pretty full.				
19. I feel that others would be better off if I were dead.				
20. I still enjoy the things I used to do.				

AN OVERVIEW OF DEPRESSION

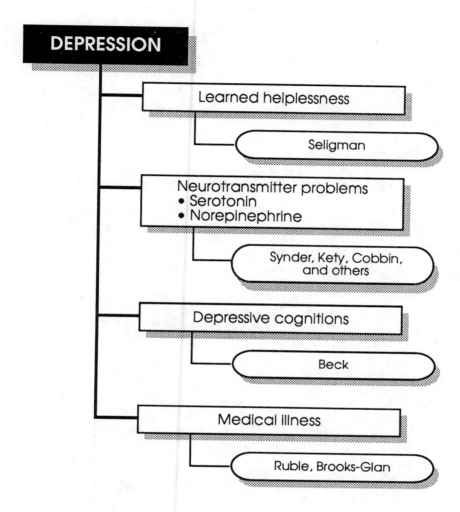

DURKHEIM'S CLASSIFICATION OF SUICIDE

Types	Etiology	Secondary Varieties
Egoistic Suicide	Apathy general depression	Indolent melancholy with self-complacence
Altruistic Suicide	Energy of passion or will	With calm feelings of duty With mystic enthusiasm With peaceful courage
Anomic Suicide	Irritation, disgust, disappointment	Violent recriminations against life in general Violent recriminations against one particular person (homicide-suicide)
Ego-Anomic Suicide		Mixture of agitation apathy, of action and revery
Anomic-Altruistic Suicide		Exasperated Effervesence
Ego-Altruistic Suicide		Melancholy tempered with moral fortitude

THE STRUGGLE OF KITTY DUKAKIS

Her bout with alcohol shows the danger of cross addiction

Anastasia Toufexis

During the presidential campaign, Kitty Dukakis stumped tirelessly for her husband, Michael. But since his loss at the polls in November, she has kept a low profile, particularly in her home state. She even failed to put in an appearance a month ago when her husband announced that he would not seek another term as Governor of Massachusetts. Last week Michael Dukakis revealed that his wife suffered from more than post-defeat blues. He explained that Kitty had checked into a private clinic in Newport, R.I., for treatment of an alcohol problem that had surfaced suddenly after the election. Said the governor: "A combination of physical exhaustion, the stress of the campaign effort and post-election letdown all combined to create a situation in which, on a limited number of occasions while at home, she has used alcohol in excessive quantities."

The announcement shocked friends and reporters, who describe Kitty as a social drinker who enjoyed a glass of wine with dinner. But the news came as no surprise to drug-abuse experts. Kitty, 52, had confessed early in the campaign to a 26 year addiction to amphetamine diet pills, a reliance she had overcome in 1982. Increasingly, counselors recognize that dependence on one substance increases the risk of abusing others.

This phenomena is known as cross-dependence, or cross addiction. Researchers estimate that between 40% and 60% of people in treatment programs are multiple-substance abusers. Sometimes people mix several drugs at once — liquor and tranquilizers, for example, as in former First Lady Betty Ford's case. Others like Kitty Dukakis, may slip from one chemical to another. Says counselor Fred Holmquist of the Hazelden Foundation in Center City, Minnesota, where Kitty was treated for amphetamine abuse: "It's like switching staterooms on the Titanic."

Why addictive tendencies cluster in some people is still a mystery. Researchers know that some sufferers have an inherited physical susceptibility to alcoholism and perhaps to abuse of other substances as well. There may also be a psychological vulnerability. Experts dismiss the popular idea that there is a set of personality traits, say, low self-esteem and a streak of perfectionism, that puts people on the path to dependency. Explains Dr. Sheila Blume, director of a treatment program at South Oaks Hospital in Amityville, N.Y.: "There is no evidence of a single addictive personality type. You cannot go to a class of junior high kids and pick out who will become an addict." Nonetheless, addicts do have a common pattern of behavior. Observes Blum: "They have translated feelings of distress like 'I'm bored" or 'I'm lonely" or 'I'm angry' into feelings of 'I need a drink' or 'a hit' or 'a fix.'" Tina Tessina, a therapist in Long Beach, California, points out that people with dependencies try to "meet their emotional needs" with alcohol or drugs.

Friends and observers agree that her husband's presidential defeat was an emotionally crushing blow to Kitty. An energetic and ambitious woman, she had thrived on the demanding schedule, tumult and attention of the campaign. Sandy Bakalar, a close friend, says "Kitty was going 1,000 miles a minute. Then on November 8 it was suddenly over. It was a terrible loss." Her husband, meanwhile, handled the loss in his usual stoic fashion. "Kitty had to do the mourning for both of them," says Richard Gaines, editor of the Boston *Phoenix*, who has long reported on the Dukakis family.

Kitty tried to put together a new life, signing a $175,000 book contract and registering with a speakers' bureau. She also traveled, taking a tip to an Arizona spa. And apparently she drank. Enough to alarm her family and, most important, herself. Doctors do not believe she has had the time to become heavily dependent on alcohol, but they say her earlier experience with amphetamines evidently set off warning bells. "She recognized that her recovery was a day-to-day thing, and she is an addictive person," says Paul Costello, her press secretary during the campaign. She has struggled mightily but unsuccessfully to stop smoking cigarettes, a habit she picked up as a teenager. On the hustings Kitty frequently talked about the dangers of drug abuse, using herself as an example.

That keen self-awareness should stand her in good stead at Edgehill, Newport, the 12 1/2 acre residential facility where she is expected to stay for about a month. Patients there are assigned to one of six 24-bed rehabilitation units. Treatment, which combines medical an psychological therapy with elements from Alcoholics Anonymous, includes intense group and peer counseling designed to break down addicts' denial of their problems. Sessions with family members are also offered.

Cross-dependent people as a rule are more difficult to treat than single-substance abusers. Often they admit to having trouble with one chemical — cocaine for example — but hide the fact that they are misusing sleeping pills or alcohol. Says Dr. Roger Meyer of the Alcohol Research Center at the University of Connecticut in Farmington: "It's hard to get them focused and to realize that they need to be talking about total abstinence from all mood-altering drugs." Kitty Dukakis has understood the message but must translate it into practice. Said her husband: "As she has now discovered, whether it comes in a bottle or is solid, if you're chemically dependent, you're chemically dependent."

Discussion Questions

1. Nicotine and caffeine have been designated as "substances"; why then are these two chemicals not identified when people talk about cross-addictions?

2. Should other forms of addictions, such as addictions to exercise, foods, religions, etc., be included in the discussion on cross- addictions given that in many incidents, physical as well as psychological damage/injury can and does occur?

Chapter 13
Therapies

AN OVERVIEW OF PSYCHOTHERAPY

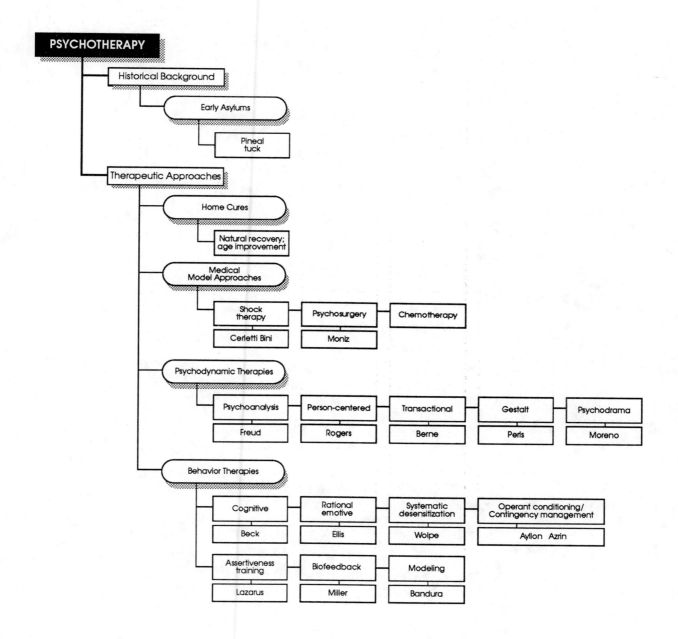

A PRIMER ON THE PROFESSIONS

Psychiatrist	a medical doctor (M.D.) who specializes in abnormal human behavior.
Psychologist	an individual who has achieved a Ph.D in psychology. Maybe a therapist, professor, or researcher.
Clinical Psychologist	has a Ph.D. in clinical psychology and specializes in the treatment of behavioral problems with some form of psychotherapy.
Counseling Psychologist	has a Ph.D in counseling psychology and tends to work more with life-adjustment problems. The distinction between clinical and counseling psychologists is not clearcut.
Clinical Social Worker **Psychiatric Social Worker**	These two professions overlap, if they are not the same thing. They require a Master's Degree in social work and two years experience in a clinical setting.
Psychoanalyst	generally a psychiatrist and a graduate of a specific psychoanalysis institute. Therapy involves some variation of psychoanalysis.
Psychotherapist	typically a clinical or counseling psychologist whose therapy is some form of psychotherapy; psychotherapy being the application of psychological knowledge to behavioral, emotional, or cognitive problems.

AN OVERVIEW OF PSYCHOANALYSIS

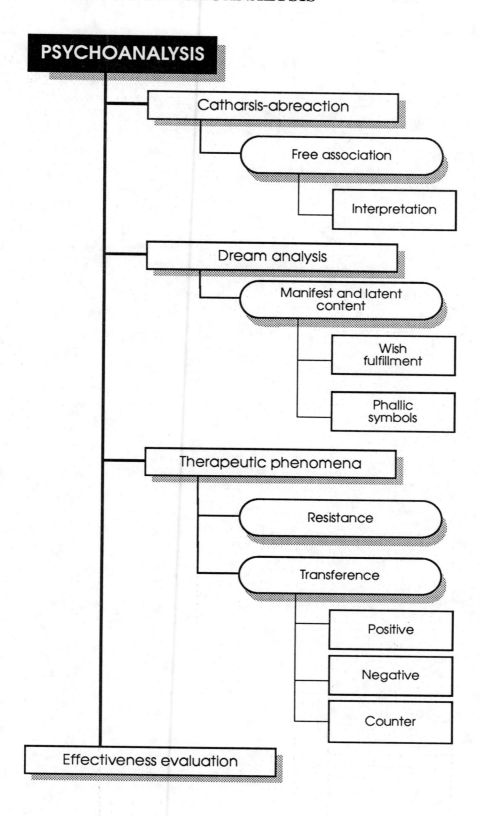

PSYCHOANALYSIS

- Catharsis-abreaction
  - Free association
    - Interpretation
- Dream analysis
  - Manifest and latent content
    - Wish fulfillment
    - Phallic symbols
- Therapeutic phenomena
  - Resistance
  - Transference
    - Positive
    - Negative
    - Counter
- Effectiveness evaluation

AN OVERVIEW OF BEHAVIOR THEORY

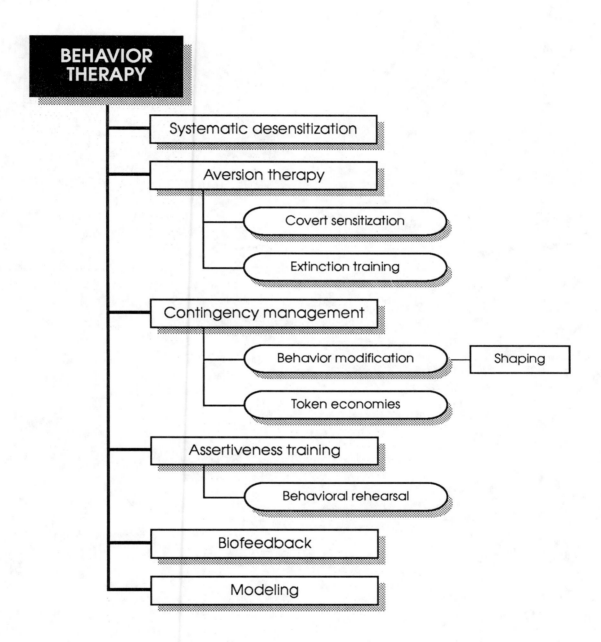

AN OVERVIEW OF COGNITIVE THERAPY

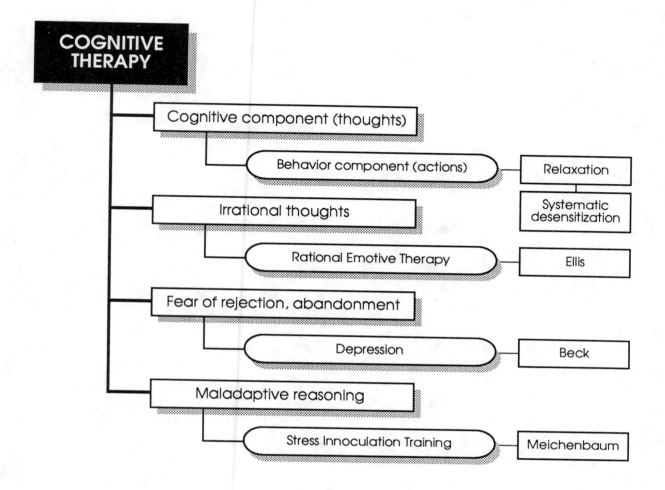

USING ASSERTIVE BEHAVIOR TO GET A JOB

One of the more critical situations in which you may find it helpful to assert yourself is the job interview. If this prospect is distressing, you can build up to it step by step, through a hierarchy of experiences that involves gradual approach and behavior rehearsal. Early successes have a way of making later goals appear less frightening.

You can break down job-seeking skills into an easy practice level, a medium practice level, and the target behavior level or actual interview:

Easy Practice Level

Read through the advertisements in newspapers. Select several positions in which you have no interest. Call the prospective employer, introduce yourself by name, indicate how you learned of the opening, request a fuller job description than the one offered in the paper, and ask for a fuller description of the qualifications desired in applicants. Thank the employer for his time, and indicate that you will get in touch if you wish to pursue application. You may also wish to ask why the position has become available — through expansion, reshuffling of personnel, employee resignation — and for information about the criteria used to determine raises and promotions.

Contact a number of friends and ask them if they are aware of any openings in your field.

Make a list of the assets and liabilities you would bring to a new job. List reliability and concern that a job gets done properly among your assets. Nonassertive people commonly have a blind spot for the value of these qualities in themselves.

Answer a newspaper advertisement for a job in which you might be interested by letter (unless telephoning is required).

Medium Practice Level

Go to your state employment office or list yourself with personnel agencies. Inform these agencies of your assets and of your preferred working conditions.

Use behavior rehearsal to practice an interview with a prospective employer. Write down a list of questions that you are likely to be asked. Include challenging questions such as why you are contemplating leaving your present position or why you are out of work. Expect to be asked what special talents or qualifications you can bring to the job. Look in the mirror and answer these questions. Maintain direct eye contact with yourself. Rehearse several statements that you will probably be able to use intact, attending to your tone of voice and bodily posture. Have a family member or confidant provide you with social feedback. Use someone who can be constructively critical, not someone who thinks that all your behavior is either perfect or beyond salvation.

Go to local businesses in person, ask for application forms, fill them out, and return them.

Write or, if possible, phone employers advertising openings in which you do have interest. Request a fuller job description by saying something like, "I wonder if you can tell me more about the opening." Indicate that you will send a resume, as required, and that you look forward to the prospect of an interview.

Target Behavior Level

After you have sent in a resume in response to an advertisement and waited for a reasonable period of time, phone the prospective employer and say, "I wonder if there is anything you can share with me about the recruitment process."

During interviews, be certain that you have had an opportunity to point out your assets for the position. Maintain direct eye contact with the interviewer. Admit freely and openly to liabilities that would become evident with the passage of time — such as lack of administrative experience in a given area. But also emphasize your capacity and interest in learning about new phases of your work. Point out your desire to "grow."

During interviews, be certain to ask what would be expected of you on a day-to-day basis. Inquire about the firm's policies for advancement and raises. Do not be afraid to inquire about the fiscal solvency of the firm. Have a few specific questions prepared that will show that you have knowledge of your field and are aware enough to wish to alert yourself to potential pitfalls in the new position. You must ask why the position has become open. If someone was unhappy with the job, you must inquire why. This inquiry need not be negativistic in tone, but failure to ask will make you appear very "hungry" for the position,

At the conclusion of an interview, thank the interviewer for his time. You may write a one- or two-line note of thanks. Indicate that you look forward to hearing from the firm. Keep it brief so that you will not appear overly anxious.

During interviews, it is normal to be nervous. If your voice cracks at some point, or if your thoughts get momentarily jumbled, say strait-forwardly that you are "somewhat nervous." This is assertive behavior. You are expressing an honest feeling.

TALK IS AS GOOD AS A PILL

John Lee

Many psychotherapists, perhaps most, believe that 1) talk therapy certainly works, but 2) no one will ever be able to prove it. Studies designed to demonstrate the effectiveness of psychotherapies have often bogged down in procedural squabbles and in doubts that anything remotely scientific can rise from such a subjective field. But now therapists have a study to cheer about; a six-year, $10 million effort concluding that talk therapy can be just as good as drug therapy in treating depression. Exultant scientists at the National Institute of Mental Health, which funded the project, hail it as a "landmark," and Psychiatrist Jerome Frank call it the "standard against which all other psychotherapy research will be assessed." Says Herbert Pardes, former director of NIMH: "It is unique in terms of size and the elegance of its construction."

Some 240 patients and 28 therapists are involved in the ongoing project at three sites: the University of Pittsburgh; the University of Oklahoma in Oklahoma City; and George Washington University in Washington. The study compares the effectiveness of two forms of brief psychotherapy with treatment by a standard antidepressant drug, imipramine. The drug got quicker results, but the talk therapies caught up after three months. By the end of the 16-week test period, all three treatments had eliminated serious symptoms of depression in more than half the patients.

So far, only a six-page summary of initial findings has been released. Describing the interim results last week at the American Psychiatric Association's annual meeting in Washington, the coordinator of the project at NIMH, Irene Elkin, said there is no evidence that drug treatment is any more effective than cognitive behavior therapy or interpersonal psychotherapy. Those therapies were chosen because they are commonly used for depression and can be readily taught to therapists from official manuals. Says Morris Parloff, a retired psychologist who helped frame the study: "We picked them because they are brief and very definable, from different approaches, and both have been tested and found effective."

Unlike Freudian treatment, which is psychodynamic and concerned with the genesis of unconscious conflict, the two talk therapies are straight-from-the-shoulder approaches dealing with the patient's current problems. Cognitive behavior therapy, the creation of Psychiatrist Aaron Beck, assumes that depression is the result of disordered patterns of thinking and tries to get patients to drop unrealistically negative views. Interpersonal psychotherapy, developed by the New Haven-Boston Collaborative Depression Project, attempts to reassure patients and improve their relationships.

All three treatments worked well with less disturbed patients, but among the severely depressed (44% of the sample), cognitive behavior therapy proved less effective than drug or interpersonal therapy. Researchers are inclined to doubt that the difference is significant. The general finding that the two different talk therapies are about equally effective strengthens the hand of those who believe that since most therapies get about the same results, the hotly debated differences among talk treatments are basically irrelevant.

The announcement of the findings comes at a time when drug treatments are on the rise and psychotherapists are under heavy pressure from health-insurance programs to find quick and cheap treatments that work. Though the art and experience of the therapist may be crucial to a cure, these are factors that hardly lend themselves to scientific analysis, which is one reason that the NIMH study chose talk therapies that can be packaged and dispensed relatively easily. The 18 therapists who conducted the two talk therapies were certified in those treatments after two years of training.

The study included a control group of patients who received placebos instead of imipramine, along with verbal support and encouragement by psychiatrists. In this group, 29% of patients lost their serious symptoms, although they had no treatment. Many depressions wax and wane or clear up on their own, and the sheer act of deciding to enter a therapy program may sometimes be more beneficial that the therapy itself. The way to catch any such brief psychological boost is in follow-up studies. The NIMH project is testing patients after six, twelve and eighteen months, with the end of the tests due by December. Three-quarters of these results are already in, but Elkin has not looked at them yet. She says she has her hands full just examining their treatment data.

Discussion Questions

1. If it is true that many depressions wax or wane or clear up on their own over time, is it possible that none of the treatments listed above really works? Disuss your thoughts/feelings.

2. The study found that medication worked faster than talk therapy, although talk therapy was as effective over time. Discuss the pros and cons (from your perspective) of using medications alone? therapy alone? and a combination of therapy and medication?

IN MASSACHUSETTS: THEATER THERAPY

David Brand

The rehearsal room is a maze of noisy motion: a woman is screaming at her stage husband, "I'm sick of your drinking, get out of the house!"; a small unshaven man cowers childlike as his "mother" delivers an obscene tongue-lashing; a man in a red-check robe staggers drunkenly as his belt whips with violent slaps against a board, while his "son" whimpers in pain; a young man sits huddled on the floor, repeating over and over, "Why doesn't anyone love me?" The air quivers with tension as the parts of the play come together and roles are refined. Tomorrow is the day of the performance, and for most of these actors the investment is not merely the sweat of creation, it is the disgorging of memories of humiliation, anger and loneliness.

This is theater of the prison cell, an unsparing, nerve-jarring mirror to the interior world of the convict. It is guided by the Geese Company, a remarkable troupe of nine young actors founded and led by a former University of Iowa drama teacher, John Bergman, 40. Since 1980 the actors have been crisscrossing the country in a rickety red-and- white bus, playing in penitentiaries and juvenile-detention centers, holding theatrical workshops and performing their largely improvised plays about prison life. One aim is to force prisoners to admit to themselves that criminal behavior is stupid and ugly. "Our work is no more than 20th century versions of medieval folk tales," says the British-born Bergman, a voluble, witty man who smokes incessantly and is forever running his hand through his tangled, shoulder-length hair.

During the performances at more than 260 prisons — whose payments for the most part support the group — the Geese have faced threats of violence and sullen silence. But the challenge in the rehearsal room at the Massachusetts Treatment Center in Bridgewater is daringly new: to use the tools of theater to break through to the feelings of the sexual deviant. The twelve inmates in the cast, like the 243 other occupants of the maximum-security facility, are serving indeterminate terms for crimes ranging from rape to child molestation.

For the three women in the Geese Company, Jill Reinier, 26, Katy Emck, 23 and Pamela Daryl, 21, it is a personal test of courage to work with men who have committed violent sexual acts against women. Admits Reinier: "As a woman I can't help feeling their crime intensely." But, says Emck, who was recruited by Bergman when the troupe visited the Edinburgh Festival last year, "you try your hardest to see past the crime and reach the mind of the man beyond."

The ground for this eight-day theater-and-therapy workshop has been prepared by a previous visit to Bridgewater in which 15 volunteer patients (as the center calls its inmates) were guided in the creation of a drama about incidents that had affected their adult lives. On this visit Bergman's task is even more complex; to dredge up memories from the ages of five to twelve and assemble them into a play. Since, as center Administrator Ian Tink notes, "90% of these patients were sexually abused as children," the hope is that by seeing themselves as victims they will realize how they have victimized others.

Most of the cast members from the earlier productions have returned to take part in Bergman's unconventional methods for trying, as Company Member Tom Swift, 25, puts it, "to open the doors onto emotions." The director begins by asking the volunteers to act out scenes from childhood. One patient portrays a child playing with toy soldiers. He says he is blowing up his mother and father with a tank. A second man is told to imagine being discussed by his parents at a cocktail party; when an actress begins playing the role of his mother, he breaks down and decides to leave the cast. On the third day, Bergman asks the patients to design a set for the play. One draws two doors labeled PAST and FUTURE. Another draws two glasses of gin labeled MINE and HIS.

From these exercises, scraps of long-forgotten incidents start to emerge from the thickets of memory: eating tomatos and then being screamed at by a shrewish mother; a father's leaving home; an overheard neighbors' conversation about a brutal father; being rejected by schoolmates. Hall (all patients' names in this article are fictitious) is responding quickly to Bergman's constant probing and badgering. "It's like a crash course in therapy — the emotions come up so quickly," he says. "At the same time, you know you're safe because it's only a play."

After four days the drama has begun to take shape, but Bergman is far from satisfied. "We need more emotion. I'm getting full resistance," he complains. In one scene, Emck must scream obscenities at Frank. "Sounds too ladylike," the director mutters; then, to Frank: "Is that how your mother sounded?" "Worse," says Frank. "Do it again," Bergman tells Emck, as the process of art imitating life is guided by the patient's recollection of a moment in a five-year-old's life.

After the patients have left for a mall, the actors analyze their progress: "He was struggling with himself. There was the constant repetition of the idea of breaking a chain." "I'm worried about him — it's so hard to see where he's operating from." "He broke down yesterday in the divorce scene." "He's coming out from the cupboard." "He wants to do a birthday-party scene in which his father dies."

Now Bergman must take this raw material, put it into some order and then "frame it to represent the world of the child." The set consists of red tubular scaffolding with connecting platforms. Around this are displayed the emblems of childhood: a red plastic baseball bat, a father's jacket, a mother's frying pan, a sister's dress and, the play's most symbolic prop, the leather strap. For three hours actors and patients work at making a whole out of their disparate scenes. What emerges is a riveting pastiche in which children are beaten by drunken parents, humiliated by everyone, and above all, forced to exist in a world of aching loneliness, a child in a wheelchair dreams of riding a bike, another child makes an imaginary phone call to a schoolmate who has rejected him. In the final scene a child is confronted by his tormentors; instead of slinking away, he turns to the audience and utters a defiant "no."

Bergman, clearly affected, declares, "This is a very powerful piece of theater, but there is still much to be resolved." The patients are also deeply moved: "John, this is very scary. There is a lot of anxiety," says one. "There are so many innuendos here," says another. There are, says the director, "ripples for us all."

The final day starts badly. The first run-through is plodding and devoid of feeling.

"Deadly," is Bergman's biting comment. Then comes another crisis: only 20 patients at the center have signed up to attend the performance, probably to protest the administration's recent tightening of security. Swift rushes away to urge all staff members to attend. Unflustered, Bergman continues his relentless demands on his cast. To Harry: "You are supposed to be a nasty human being." To everyone: "I want more feeling; we've got to have some life."

The director is struggling against the prisoners' last-minute reluctance to reveal too much about themselves. But his harangue has its effect, and the two performances, given largely to staff, are intense and deeply felt. During one, a patient in the audience, overcome by emotion, rushes out. Another sits, tears streaming down his face. Says a therapist: "More has come out in this performance than in months of therapy."

Some of the patients have come close to understanding the roots of their turmoil. All are emotionally exhausted. One patient, a man with horn-rimmed glasses and a pendulous stomach, sits weeping. Others embrace. An actress is unable to hold back the tears. Ted speaks for many of his fellow patients when he says, "For the first time I have something to wake up for in the morning."

Discussion Questions

1. Given what you know about personalities and therapies, do you feel that Bergman's approach is ethical? Why?

2. Compare and contrast Bergman's approach to Freud's (psychoanalysis), Rogers's (humanistic), and Rotter's (social learning).

Chapter 14
Human Sexuality

AN OVERVIEW OF HUMAN SEXUALITY

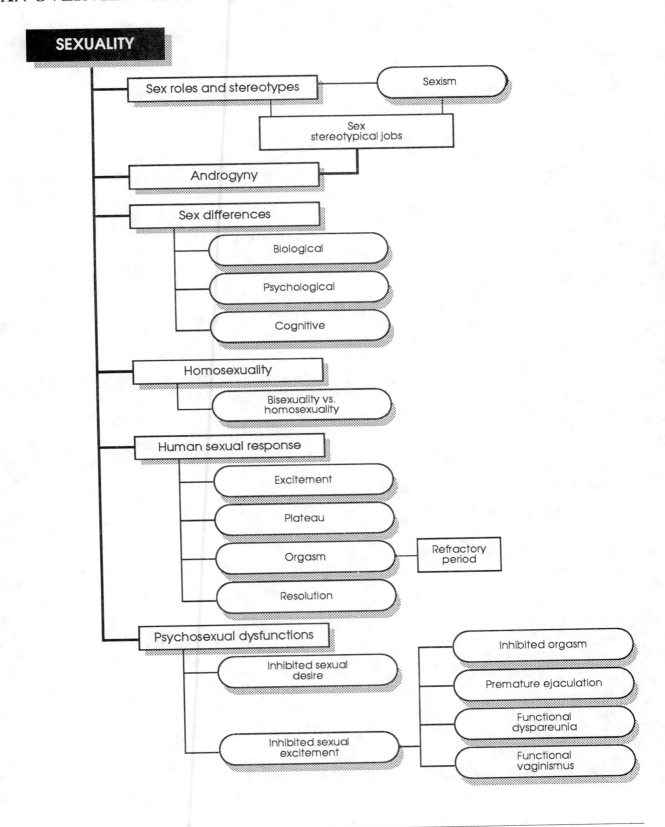

MALE AND FEMALE SEXUAL RESPONSE PATTERNS

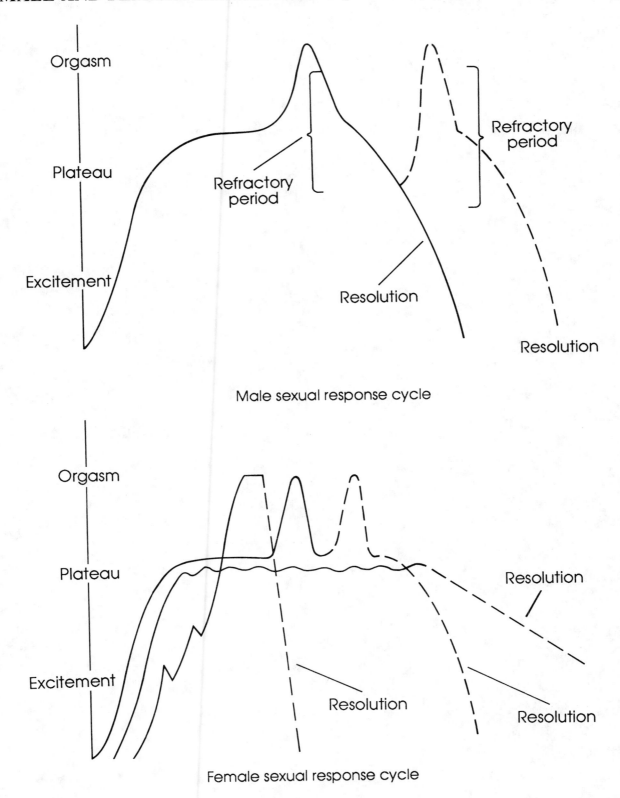

Male sexual response cycle

Female sexual response cycle

ON THE TRAIL OF THE BIG O

John Leo

Ralph and Wanda ponder the peripatetic pleasure zone.

Ralph: Quiz time, dearest. What moves around more often than Elizabeth Taylor, the QE2 and the wandering albatross?

Wanda: I give up, Ralph. What?

Ralph: The female orgasm. In the old days, it used to be in the vagina. Then they moved it to the clitoris, where it remained stationary for a decade. Now it seems to be on the move again. Just restless, I guess.

Wanda: Ralph, what on earth are you talking about?

Ralph: The Great Traveling Orgasm, my pet. Under the majestic scepter of science, not to mention the cattle prod of sexual politics, the Big O is thrashing about once again. It's gone from vagina to clitoris and now seems headed for the brain and back to the vagina. Before you know it, it will come to rest on the elbow of the pancreas. Ralph's *Guide to Sex,* as yet unpublished, will advise all ardent males to rub everything once. One never knows where tomorrow's sexual climaxes will be located.

Wanda: I am about to have an out-of-body experience, Ralph. But I suppose I could remain here with you and your monologue if a fact or two happened to intrude.

Ralph: Facts are the backbone of good argument, my beloved. I hold here in my hand the current winter issue of the *Journal of Sex & Marital Therapy.* I quote: "From recent empirical studies it can be concluded that most (and probably all) women possess vaginal zones whose tactile stimulation can lead to orgasm." Apparently the long tyranny of the clitoris is coming to an end, dearest. At least until the next dramatic break-through of sexual science or the next wave of feminism.

Wanda: You argue like a rogue elephant runs, Ralph. Look, Masters and Johnson showed that the clitoral–vaginal debate was irrelevant. There is only one kind of orgasm, and it almost always involves stimulation of the clitoris. It's just that orgasms without that stimulation are rarer and milder than those with it.

Ralph: Manfully argued, my pet. But let us cast a practiced eye at the politics of orgasm. Freud thought that truly mature women always shift their focus from the clitoris to the vagina, so women who needed clitoral stimulation were made to feel like retards or perverts. The feminists just reversed that. It was a much-loved way of downgrading penis–vagina sex and upgrading masturbation. Soon provagina women had to take to the hills like guerrillas. Clitoral enforcers like Shere Hite were sent out to mop up any remaining opposition: the poor deluded women who said they had vaginal orgasms and thought they were enjoying them. Hite called this "emotional" orgasm, as opposed to "real" orgasm. The clitoro-feminists also managed to clear out the compromisers, who believed in "blended" vaginal–clitoral orgasms. What the heck. It worked for Scotch, why not climaxes? But no, the clitoral-pride movement got so strong it became somewhat embarrassing to admit that you owned a vagina or a penis. For all we know, women who used to fake vaginal orgasms for their hubbies began to fake clitoral ones for the women's movement. I guess you could call this progress of a sort. But do women really have to limit themselves to politically correct orgasms? Wanda, I stand before you as that rarest of males, a true feminist, calling for relief from the dogmas of Freudians and clitorists alike!

Wanda: I liked you better as a chauvinist pig, husband of mine. Your argument has only one minor flaw, Ralph: it's totally wrong. There is no clitoral party line, though easily threatened males may think so. The clitoris is the normal center of women's sexuality, and it is not our fault that it happens to be located in a spot that men find inconvenient. I bet that the article in the *Journal* of *Sex & Marital Therapy* is just more woolgathering about the G spot.

Ralph: Wrong, beloved helpmate. In fact, the author of the journal's piece, a sexologist named Heli Alzate, says that his own studies show no evidence of any such sexually sensitive tissues in the vaginal wall where the G spot is alleged to be. These are dark days for G spotologists, my dear. Ernst Grafenberg discovered his spot in the late '40's. But after many exhausting years in the lab stimulating all those hired prostitutes and cutting up all those cadavers, there's still no convincing evidence. But then, sexology is not an exact science. Who says sexologists should be able to locate a major sexual organ after only 40 years of searching? Anyway, the G spot people say the sensitive spot is usually found between 11 o'clock and 1 o'clock on the vaginal barrel. Alzate thinks there may be two other hot spots, at 4 o'clock and 8 o'clock.

Wanda: Why do I find all this so tacky? All these white-coated males poking around the female body, checking the wiring and looking for new buttons to push. Why are you all so obsessed with the technology of women's bodies?

Ralph: Easy, Wanda. It's just that males found out where their orgasms were located a million years ago, and women are still working on it. They'll probably figure it out any day now. No offense. It's just that if men's bodies were constructed like that, we'd still be looking for our knees.

Wanda: Let me tell you a little secret, Ralph. I married a lout. Who cares about the technology of orgasm? Sex is supposed to be part of a relationship, not a high school biology course. Some women have orgasms without contractions, and the white coats smile and say, "Sorry, we can't count those because we can't measure them." Same old stuff of males using science to define and control women.

Ralph: Mellow out, dearest. Surely an acknowledged feminist such as myself is not the enemy . . .

Wanda: I'm developing a blinding headache in my R spot. That's tiny part of my brain that thinks you're rational, Ralph. This headache is fully located between 9 p.m. and 6 a.m. on both my clock and my cranial barrel. Thank you and good night.

PSYCHOSEXUAL DISORDERS

Gender Identity Disorders

Transsexualism
Gender identity disorder of childhood
Atypical gender identity disorder

Paraphilias

Exhibitionism
Fetishism
Atypical Frotteurism
Pedophilia
Sexual masochism
Sexual sadism
Transvestic fetishism
Voyeurism

Psychosexual Dysfunctions

Hypoactive sexual desire
Sexual aversion disorder
Female sexual arousal disorder
Male erectile disorder
Inhibited female orgasm
Inhibited male orgasm
Premature ejaculation
Dysparevnia vaginismus

Other Psychosexual Disorders

Ego-dystonic homosexuality
Psychosexual disorders not elsewhere classified

LOVE, SEX, AND YOU

A Quiz on AIDS

1. Who can get AIDS?

   a. Gay men
   b. Anyone
   c. IV drug users

2. Which of these will NOT spread AIDS?

   a. Sharing a hot tub or swimming pool
   b. Having intercourse without a condom
   c. Donating blood
   d. Sharing needles in drug use
   e. Mosquito bites

3. Can you tell by looking at someone whether he or she is infected with the AIDS virus?

   a. Yes
   b. No
   c. Sometimes (Explain): _____

   _____

   _____

4. What is one way to reduce your risk for catching AIDS?

   a. Make sure your sexual partner looks healthy
   b. Don't hug IV drug users
   c. Limit your number of sex partners
   d. Don't go swimming in a public pool

5. What is safer sex?

   a. Look for sores or spots on your partner's body
   b. Don't exchange blood, semen, or vaginal secretions
   c. Only have sex once in a while
   d. None of the above

6. Which ways can the AIDS virus be transmitted?

   a. On toilet seats
   b. College athletes who use steroids and share needles
   c. Eating in a cafeteria with someone who has AIDS
   d. Intimate sexual contact
   e. Hugging or touching someone with AIDS

7. Do most college students use condoms when having sex?

    a. Yes
    b. No
    c. Sometimes (Explain): _____

    _____

    _____

8. A woman who once used IV drugs stopped doing so about two years ago. She feels perfectly healthy. Does she need to worry about the possibility of her sexual partner getting AIDS from her?

    a. Yes
    b. No

9. Which of these activities might expose you to the AIDS virus?

    a. Eating in a restaurant that employs a gay cook
    b. Having more than one sex partner
    c. Using a public drinking fountain

10. Some people are at increased risk for AIDS. These would include

    a. Women
    b. Blacks or Hispanics
    c. Teenagers
    d. Babies born to parents who use IV drugs

11. If a woman is using the birth control pill, she doesn't need to use a condom when having sex.

    a. True
    b. False
    c. Sometimes (Explain:) _____

    _____

    _____

12. What local resources are available for AIDS and STD (sexually transmitted disease) information and/or medical care?

    _____

    _____

    _____

13. A negative test result for the AIDS virus means you are not infected.

    a. True
    b. False

Answers to AIDS Quiz

1. B   While gays and IV drug users are the highest risk populations, anyone can contract AIDS.

2. A, E   To date, the only known way to contract or transmit AIDS is through sexual activities or sharing IV needles.

3. B   While there are definite symptoms associated with AIDS, e.g., weight loss, fatigue, chronic cough, etc., these symptoms are also indicative of other diseases and problems.

4. C   Limit the number, and practice safe sex.

5. B   Safer sex is using condoms at all times, which prevents the exchange of blood, semen, and vaginal secretions, and limiting the number of sexual partners.

6. B, B   Again, AIDS can only be transmitted sexually or through the sharing of IV needles.

7. B   Recent statistics on the spread of AIDS would suggest that a number of people are not using condoms — among those groups, college students are showing an increase in the number of diagnosed cases of AIDS.

8. A   AIDS has an incubation period of 7–10 years.

9. B

10. A, B, C, D

11. B   The AIDS virus passes with the exchange of semen and vaginal secretions, which are unaffected by the use of birth control pills.

12.   Look these up in your local telephone directory and list them.

13. B   While the tests today are becoming more sophisticated and more accurate, we continue to have false negative and false positive results.

LATEST INFERTILITY SUSPECT: CAFFEINE

For women trying to become pregnant, a growing list of dos and don'ts accompanies the standard morning temperature readings and ovulation charts. Gain a few pounds if you're slender. Lose if you're overweight. Stop exercising intensively. Don't smoke tobacco or marijuana. Now the latest: cut down on coffee, cola, and chocolate. Moderate caffeine consumption, a recent study of 104 women has found, may lessen the chance of conception by as much as 50 percent.

In the first statistical evaluation of the effects of caffeine on fertility, researchers at the National Institutes of Health found that women who drank more than one cup of coffee (or two and a half soft drinks) a day were "consistently less likely to become pregnant" than their counterparts who consumed less. Fertility experts point out that the study is small, of limited scope, and does not prove conclusively that caffeine significantly affects fertility. The authors themselves insist the results must be "interpreted with caution." But if a patient has medically unexplained infertility, says Dr. Benjamin Younger of the American Fertility Society, cutting down on caffeine consumption "is a reasonable thing to do." At the very least, the possibility of a caffeine–fertility link should provide coffee drinkers, cola nuts, and chocoholics with plenty of food for thought.

Discussion Questions

1. Should the manufacturers of coffee be made to place a warning on the coffee can/ jar label regarding the possible effects on fertility?

2. Should there be a national coffee campaign similar to those warning about the negative effects of alcohol and nicotine on unborn babies? Why?

BIRTH CONTROL
New approval for a 19th-century technique

Matt Clark

What do women want? For one thing, they want more choices of contraceptive method. The two most effective ones present nettlesome problems: the Pill may cause nausea and other unpleasant side effects, and can increase the risk of blood-clot problems and strokes. The IUD has largely disappeared because a series of multi-million-dollar lawsuits over injuries attributed to the devices prompted manufacturers to stop making them. Last week U.S. women got another choice for birth control: the U.S. Food and Drug Administration approved sale of the cervical cap, a contraceptive invented in the 19th century and long available in Europe.

The cap is a small, thimble-shaped device made of latex that is placed directly over the cervix. Before insertion, the user places only a small amount of spermicidal cream or jelly within the cap. According to the FDA approval, the cap can be kept in place without the need for additional application of spermicide for at least 48 hours, although many women have worn it in clinical trials for at least three days. By contrast, most doctors recommend that the diaphragm be left in place no longer than 24 hours, and that additional spermicidal jelly or cream be added before another act of intercourse takes place. " We think the cap is particularly appropriate for younger women who can put it in on Friday and their contraception is taken care of until Monday morning," says Victoria Leonard, executive director of the National Women's Health Network.

The cap and the diaphragm are about equally effective. In a study involving more than 1,000 women, Dr. Gerald Bernstein of the University of Southern Medical Center found that the pregnancy rate among those using the cap was 17.4 % compared with 16.7% among women using the diaphragm. About 4% of women using the cap in clinical trials showed abnormal cells in Pap smears after three months, as compared to 1.7% among diaphragm wearers. These abnormal cells, however, don't necessarily portend cancer. As a condition of approval, the FDA advises that the cap should only be prescribed to women with normal Pap smear results, and that users undergo a follow-up test after three months.

Until now it has been kept off the U.S. market, in part by stricter controls placed on contraceptive devices by Congress in the wake of the scandal involving the Dalkon Shield IUD. Feminists, led by the Women's Health Network, lobbied for the past seven years to win the FDA's approval. Now that it's here, will many women use it? Dr. Louise Tyrer of the Planned Parenthood Federation of America points out that the diaphragm ranks only fourth among contraceptive methods, behind sterilization, the Pill and condoms. "A method requiring a woman to put something in her vagina isn't popular," she says.

Meanwhile, another contraceptive choice will soon be available to U.S. women. Gyno-Pharma, Inc., of Somerville, N.J., has started marketing a new IUD. Called the ParaGard Model T 380A, it is similar to the famous Copper T, which was taken off the market two years ago because of lawsuits filed against its manufacturer. Gyno-

Pharma hopes to avert potential legal problems by requiring all women who purchase the device to initial each section of a long "consent" form listing the potential risks it entails.

Discussion Questions

1. In light of the controversy around the Pill and the IUD, what type of pre-release experiments/trials do you believe should be conducted for the Cap? The ParaGard?

2. Should there be an age restriction for the purchase of the cervical cap? ParaGard?

3. Should the cervical cap and/or ParaGard be made available at no cost to women in much the same way that the Pill has been made available?

4. Discuss your reactions to Gyno-Pharma's decision to have women who purchase the ParaGard to sign a consent form. Do you feel that this consent should protect them from litigation related to injuries caused by the ParaGrd.

Chapter 15
Social Psychology

AN OVERVIEW OF ATTITUDES

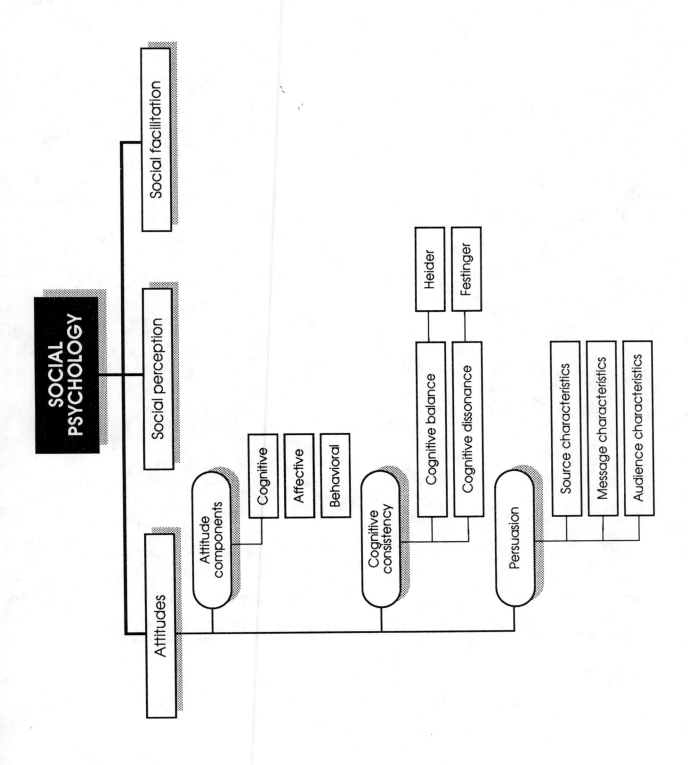

SOCIAL PERCEPTION SURVEY

Take a look at the four people pictured below—persons A, B, C, and D—and then rate them according to the scales underneath. For instance, if you find person A to be extremely poised, place the letter A in the space next to "poised." If you find person A to be extremely awkward, place the A next to "awkward." If A impresses you as being equally poised or awkward, or if you are unsure, place the A in the center space. Once you have rated person A on the fourteen scales, repeat the process for persons B, C, and D. It is perfectly permissible to place more than one letter in the same space. This will simply mean that you gave two or more people similar ratings on the scales.

poised	_____ _____ _____ _____ _____ _____ _____	awkward
modest	_____ _____ _____ _____ _____ _____ _____	vain
strong	_____ _____ _____ _____ _____ _____ _____	weak
interesting	_____ _____ _____ _____ _____ _____ _____	boring
self-assertive	_____ _____ _____ _____ _____ _____ _____	submissive
sociable	_____ _____ _____ _____ _____ _____ _____	unsociable
independent	_____ _____ _____ _____ _____ _____ _____	dependent
warm	_____ _____ _____ _____ _____ _____ _____	cold
genuine	_____ _____ _____ _____ _____ _____ _____	artificial
kind	_____ _____ _____ _____ _____ _____ _____	cruel
exciting	_____ _____ _____ _____ _____ _____ _____	dull
sexually warm	_____ _____ _____ _____ _____ _____ _____	sexually cold
sincere	_____ _____ _____ _____ _____ _____ _____	insincere
sensitive	_____ _____ _____ _____ _____ _____ _____	insensitive

Done? All right, now answer a few questions. Which man (A or D) and which woman (B or C) will be:

More likely to hold a prestigious job?	A or D? B or C?
More likely to be divorced?	A or D? B or C?
More likely to be a good parent?	A or D? B or C?
More likely to experience deep personal fulfillment?	A or D? B or C?

A

B

C

D

Source: Photos reprinted from *Adjustment and Growth: The Challenges of Life* by Spencer Rathus and Jeffrey Nevid. Copyright 1980 by Holt, Rinehart and Winston. Reprinted by permission of CBS College Publishing.

AN OVERVIEW OF SOCIAL PERCEPTION

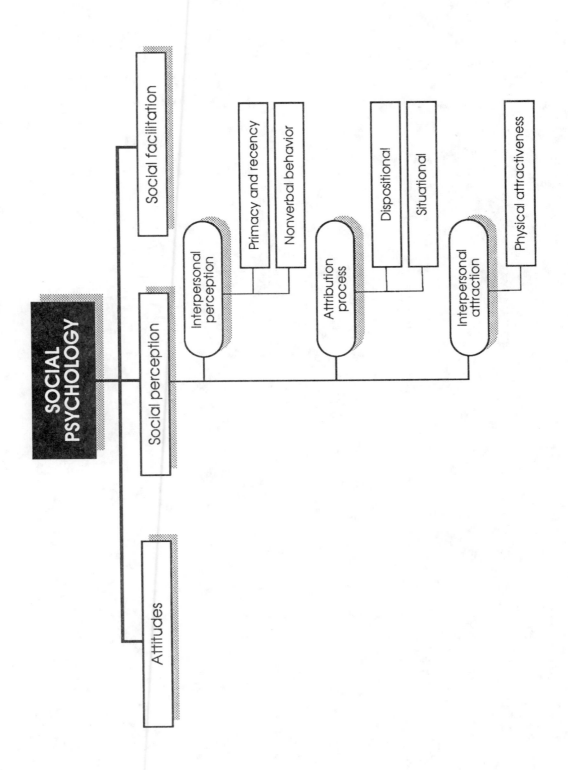

AN OVERVIEW OF SOCIAL FACILITATION

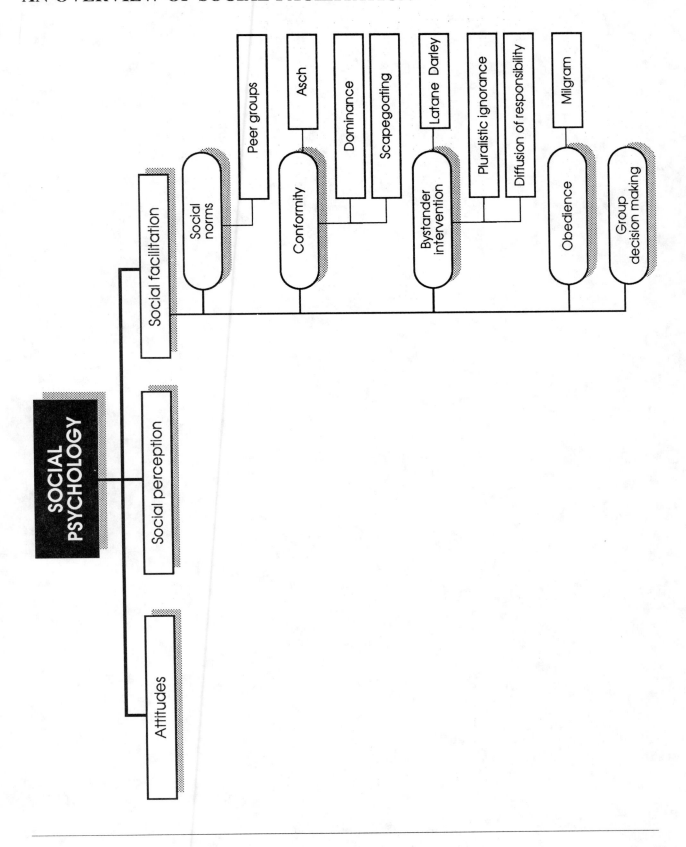

MIND IF I CUT IN ?

Vincent Bozzi

You're standing in line and someone rudely edges his way in. Do you physically hurtle him to the end of the line or do you fume quietly? It all depends on where you're standing.

The late psychologist Stanley Milgram and colleagues had people daringly break into 129 lines at railroad ticket counters, betting parlors and other New York City locations. The lines averaged six persons in length, and the "intruders" always butted in between the third and fourth person.

Suprisingly, even in New York less than half of the intruders received any objection from those already in line. Lest this finding serve as an invitation to other rude intruders, let them be forewarned that in certain circumstances line-cutters were rebuffed up to 91 percent of the time.

"The responses ranged from physical ejection of the intruder to total indifference," the researchers say.

Physical action occurred in 10 percent of the lines. "This included tugging at the sleeve or tapping the shoulder or, in a few cases, pushing the intruder firmly out of the line."

Verbal objections were the most common reaction, occurring 22 percent of the time. Typically, they said, "Excuse me, you have to go to the back of the line," or more forcefully, "No way! The line's back there." Dirty looks, hostile stares and gestures occurred in about 15 percent of the lines.

If you want to cut into a line the people in front won't give you much trouble — they objected only 27 percent of the time, compared with 73 percent for those in back.

Sometimes the researchers planted others in line to serve as "buffers" who wouldn't raise their voice if someone cut in front of them. This allowed the researchers to see what people farther back in line might do. Without buffers, 73 percent of the cutters were expelled, but if the first person did not object only 25 percent were expelled.

Discussion Questions

1. What is your response to people who cut in line in front of you? In back of you?

2. Discuss why you think the presence of "buffers" dramatically reduced the percentage of cutters who were expelled from line.

Chapter 16
Applied Psychology

AN OVERVIEW OF APPLIED PSYCHOLOGY

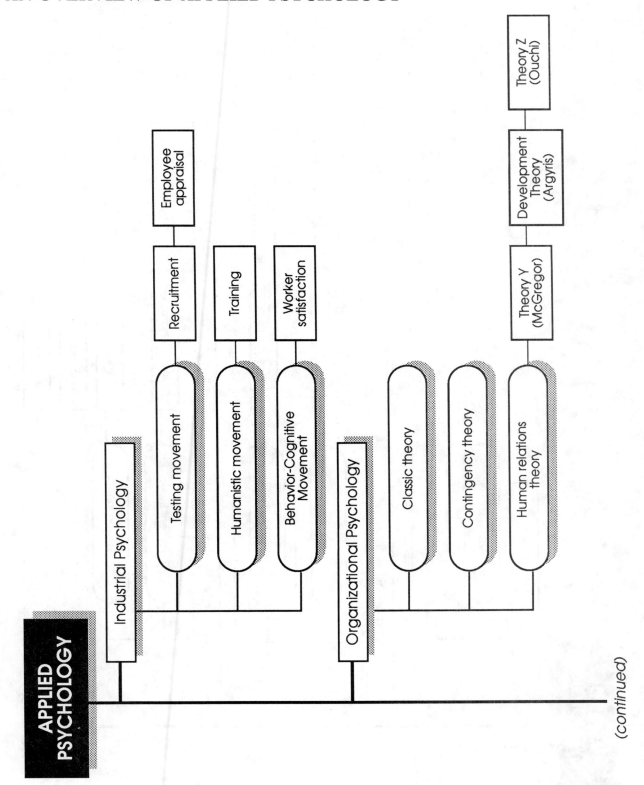

(continued)

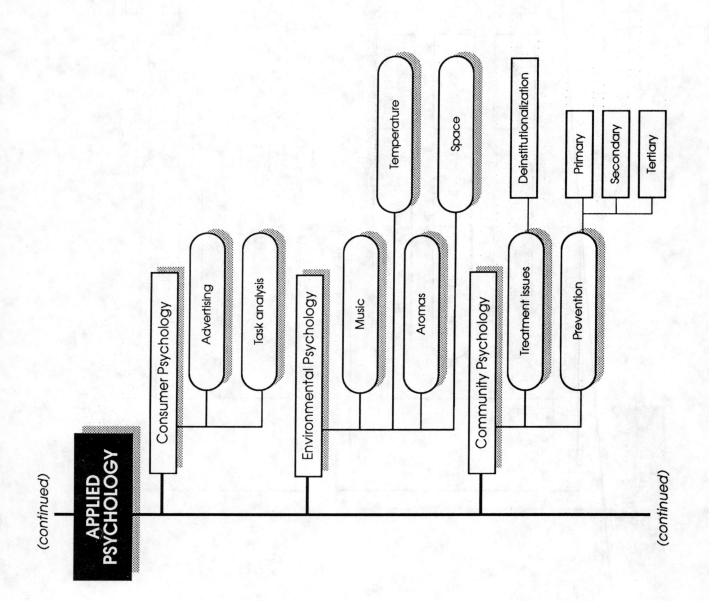

(continued)

(continued)

(continued)

APPLIED PSYCHOLOGY

Forensics Psychology
- Criminal behavior
  - Insanity plea

Sports Psychology
- Task analysis
  - Positive mental imagery

Eductional Psychology
- Teaching styles
  - Discovery
  - Exposition
- Classroom management
  - Self-fulfilling prophecy
- Measurement & evaluation
  - Grades
  - Tests
    - Norm referenced
      - Criterion referenced

THE MORAL IMPLICATIONS OF NUTRITIONAL THERAPY

Is controlling behavior through diet a humanistic alternative to incarceration?

Deane Chinen

In this country alone, one in every five Americans has been arrested for charges more serious than traffic violations, and nearly 640,000 — one in every 350 — are currently serving time in overcrowded prisons, according to Andrea Dorfman writing in the October 1984 *Science Digest.* The statistics are quite striking, yet the public seldom takes notice. What drives people to commit such reprehensible acts that they must be isolated from society and shut behind bars? No one seems to think twice about it. But crime is a major determinant damaging our society, and something must be done to cease its power.

Until recently, crime was thought to be the result of offenders' social circumstances. Broken family ties, racism, poverty, and unemployment are just some of the critical values that seem to change American citizens into criminals. However, with advances in genetics and neurology, recent studies have shown that, along with social implications, inborn chemical imbalances may underlie criminal behavior. Thus, to dissolve crime, society must start where the problem begins — with the criminal.

While genes influence what we are, it is our chemistry that affects our demeanor. Gerald Brown, a biological psychiatrist at the National Institute of Mental Health has discovered 5- hydroxyindoleacetic acid (5-HIAA), a metabolic byproduct found in the spinal fluid. It has been found that aggressive animals have consistently low levels of 5-HIAA, and Brown uncovered the same condition in men who have been aggressive and have demonstrated impulsive behavior since childhood. This connection between low 5-HIAA levels and a history of aggressive behavior has had a strong relationship. Brown can now predict, with 85 percent accuracy, which individuals in a group of servicemen would be discharged from the service for bad or unsuitable conduct, according to Dorfman.

An additional source of deviant behavior has been found in people with low blood sugar levels, or hypoglycemia. When sugar is eaten, it quickly enters the bloodstream and causes the release of insulin. Insulin is a hormone necessary for the absorption of blood sugar by most cells. However, an overabundance can plunge blood-sugar too low. If this reaches a certain baseline, the brain does not get enough energy to operate at the maximum level of efficiency. The primitive brain which controls our emotions then takes priority, and violence may result.

The two aforementioned chemical imbalances (5-HIAA and insulin) are both links to criminality. But they must be brought together by one essential link — nutrition. Foods provide many substances which influence brain chemistry and, ultimately, behavior. Therefore, researchers believe that through nutritional therapy — a moderation of the diet — body chemistry can be restored to normal. For example, a diet may be supplemented with vitamins and minerals or restricted of junk foods which are loaded with sucrose and refined carbohydrates. The results of such therapy programs are very impressive.

Researcher Angelo Lewis reports that in Dougherty County, Georgia, nutritional therapy was used to treat juvenile offenders. Biochemical tests and nutritional supplements were given to correct chemical imbalances. According to Lewis, this program eventually caused the number of serious crimes committed by juveniles in the county to drop to less than it was ten years before that time.

Criminologist Stephen Schoenthaler of the California State University-Stanislaus in Turlock also used a nutritional therapy program in fourteen juvenile institutions across the nation. He substituted fruit juices and nutritious snacks for soft drinks and high-sugar junk foods. Antisocial behavior, assaults, fights, and thefts then dropped 50 percent, Lewis reports.

Nutritional therapy has been highly praised by many, claims Dorfman. "I think nutrition therapy will become one of the main forms of treatment," says one researcher who is experimenting with neurotransmitter precursors. "There's no risk associated with it. We're not controlling behavior. We're just stimulating natural checks and balances so they can take over again."

But nutritional therapy, just like anything else, has its drawbacks. Unlike infections, chemical imbalances cannot be cured permanently. Nutritional therapy must be maintained throughout life to be efficiently usable. "It's kind of spooky," William Walsh, a researcher at the Health Research Institute notes in Dorfman's report, "you can turn them on and off with the pills."

Because "it's kind of spooky," as Walsh puts it, nutritional therapy cannot be proficiently put to use. If faulty body chemistry does indeed lie at the root of criminality, what can or should be done? And if criminality can be reversed by tinkering with chemistry, who should have such power?

Any answers raise profound questions of ethics and civil rights. Dorfman cites Robert Thatcher, a neuroscientist at the Applied Neuroscience Research Institute: "There's a gap between the traditional view of society and the new fields of neuroscience and biopsychology which have powerful techniques for diagnosing, probing, and measuring," he says. "The gap is so large that these techniques aren't being vigorously applied. There is a basic political and philosophical opposition."

Along with that, there is still a basic fear which lies in the possibility that nutritional therapy may be abused. If information on nutritional therapy was put together on a national basis, anyone would have access to using it. Thus, it could result in terrible aftereffects. So, with the numerous controversies involved, tinkering with chemistry is not widely favored.

In actuality, the scientific community on the whole feels that this kind of practical work is still premature and unsupported by sound science. Dr. Gregory E. Gray of the University of Southern California once announced, "It's nothing more than a pseudoscience." And Lewis further reports that other professionals in the science field feel that such theories are being applied by practitioners as preliminary findings and suggestions before they are even confirmed as fact.

Yet, there are still a number of practitioners who are willing to bravely take on scientific criticism, hostile editors, and whoever else opposes them. They are convinced that these programs are effective. "They said the same thing with cancer,"

Barbara Reed, a supporter of nutritional therapy, states in Lewis's report. "They said that there was absolutely no relationship between cancer and diet."

However, every argument has its compromise. There is new hope for redirecting research dealing with the causes of crime in ways able to take into account the interaction of biological and social factors. Some individuals, such as criminologist Marvin E. Wolfgang and his colleagues at the University of Pennsylvania, are already exploring these issues by analyzing social and biological factors at large. Still, more needs to be done.

It took years of patiently following the life histories of many men and women to conclude that an accurate link exists between smoking or diet and disease. It will once again take many tedious years to unravel the complexities of nutritional therapy. Nevertheless, it will soon be realized that it truly is not cost-effective to concentrate on building larger and larger prisons to care for these individuals deemed hopeless by society. And humanistically, it must be envisioned that, if changing the basic chemistry of criminals proves effective, society in its part must give these individuals a chance — a chance to live productive lives in our continuously flourishing society.

Source: Originally published in the January/February 1988 issue of The Humanist. Reprinted by permission.

Discussion Questions

1. Reflecting back on the article, respond to the questions: If faulty body chemistry does indeed lie at the root of criminality, what can or should be done? And if criminality can be reversed by tinkering with chemistry, who should have such power?

2. Do you think that it is a civil rights violation to impose a diet, nutritionally healthy or not, upon a person simply because they have been convicted of a crime?

3. Is nutrition therapy a realistic alternative to prison for juvenile delinquents? for persons convicted of misdemeanors? for persons convicted of crimes of passion? Why?

Chapter 17
Statistics

AN OVERVIEW OF STATISTICS

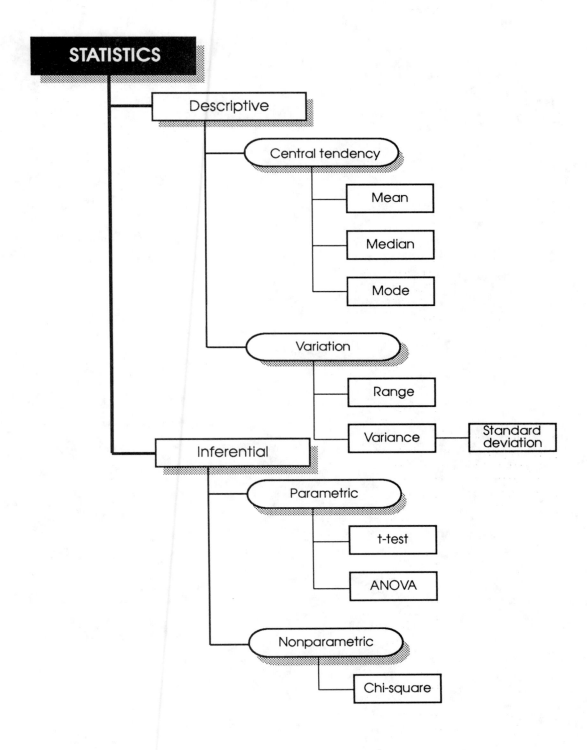

THE NORMAL DISTRIBUTION

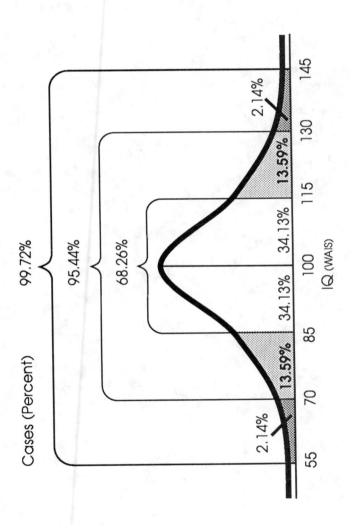